ANGEL
···· IN MY ····
ATTIC
DEVOTIONS
FOR JUNIOR HIGH GIRLS

MARY LOU CARNEY

ZondervanPublishingHouse
Grand Rapids, Michigan
A Division of HarperCollinsPublishers

Angel in My Attic
Copyright © 1988, 1992 by Mary Lou Carney

Requests for information should be addressed to:
Zondervan Publishing House
Grand Rapids, Michigan 49530

Library of Congress Cataloging-in-Publication Data

Carney, Mary Lou, 1949–
    Angel in my attic : devotions for junior-high girls / by Mary Lou
  Carney. — [New ed.]
      p. cm.
    Summary: A collection of daily devotions, accompanied by appropriate
Bible verses, in which a junior high school girl discusses with her
guardian angel troublesome aspects of Christian life for someone her
age.
    ISBN 0-310-28611-5 (pbk.)
    1. Teenage girls—Prayer-books and devotions—English. 2. Devotional
calendars. 3. Junior high school students—Prayer-books and devotions
—English. [1. Prayer books and devotions. 2. Christian life.] I. Title.
BV4551.2.C34   1992
242'.633—dc20
                                            92-305
                                              CIP
                                              AC

Edited by Pamela Hartung and Dave Lambert
Interior designed by Dave Lambert
Cover designed by Larry Taylor
Cover and interior illustrations by Matt Mew

Printed in the United States of America

93 94 95 96 / CH / 11 10 9

for Melva,
who taught me to climb
barbed wire fences
and
saved me from
the sows

This is a book of daily devotions . . .

It may not *look* like a devotional book, and it certainly doesn't *read* like one.

But it is.

We wanted to give you a different kind of devotional book. We thought you'd have more fun with it. And we thought you'd be interested in K.C., too—a middle-school girl just like you with the same problems you have, from worrying about her looks and her future to getting into trouble with her teachers at school.

You don't have a Herbie in your life—at least not that you can see and talk to. We just made him up.

But we hope Herbie and K.C.—two made-up characters—will help you to think about a God who is real. And about how that God can make a difference in the everyday, middle-school problems *you* face.

Day 1

The attic smelled of new paint and wallpaper paste. Sunlight played on the window, making the panes of old glass look curvy and thick, like Grandma's glasses. Grandma! K.C. kicked the box of books sitting just inside the door. "If it weren't for her, I wouldn't have to move up here," K.C. said aloud, her voice echoing in the empty room.

"Look out above!" Joshua's call was muffled by the big rag rug he carried on his shoulder. He helped K.C. unroll it on the wooden floor. "This is going to be a great room, sis," he said, giving her shoulder a playful punch and starting back downstairs.

"Right," K.C. said, stomping on a lump in the rug. "If you like looking at the tops of trees!"

Suddenly, the room seemed to tingle with the tinkling sound of wind chimes. K.C. whirled around. "Who's there?" She could see slants of sun making patterns on the rug. Silence. Everything looked just the same, but K.C. could *feel* something watching her. Without turning her head, she glanced toward the window. Nothing. Outside stretched the fields of her father's farm—the corn tall and thick-bladed, the soybeans green and heavy. *Tinkle-clink, tinkle-clink.* That noise! K.C. swallowed hard. "Anybody there?" A cloud passed over the sun, and the room took on a blue

dimness. Then the sound of wind chimes came again, and K.C. bolted down the attic steps.

DEAR DIARY, K.C. wrote as she sat propped up in the middle of her big, four-poster bed. TONIGHT WILL BE MY FIRST NIGHT IN MY NEW ROOM—IF YOU CAN CALL AN ATTIC A ROOM. She chewed the end of her pencil eraser and looked around. SEEMS ALMOST LIKE A REAL BEDROOM, NOW THAT I AM SURROUNDED BY ALL MY THINGS.

" 'Surrounded' has two r's," a voice close to her ear said.

K.C. jumped out of bed and stood staring at the spot where she had been sitting. All she saw was the crumpled quilt and her opened diary.

"Of course, it *is* only a diary entry," the voice went on. "Still, Mrs. Martin told you she wants you to work on your spelling."

K.C. could hear her heart beating hard in her ears, like galloping horse hooves. "Who said that?" she demanded. *Tinkle-Clink. Tinkle-Clink.* The wind chimes again!

"I did, of course."

Something was here with her. A ghost—it must be a ghost!

K.C. scanned the room. Nothing seemed different. But someone—or *something*—was here with her. A ghost—it must be a ghost! And suddenly K.C. was angry. "Show yourself, you cowardly ghost," she said. "I've been run out of one bedroom, and I'm not about to budge from this one!" The attic was thick with silence. "Go haunt somewhere else!" K.C. yelled up at the ceiling.

"Listen, kid," the voice said. "I have no intention of 'haunting'—not here, not anywhere."

It was then K.C. saw him—standing on the window sill, sunbeams dancing around his white robe and huge wings. "Who—*what* are you?"

The tiny creature stood erect and, tipping his halo, said, "Herbekiah's the name, but you can call me Herbie. And it seems rather obvious that I'm an angel—a guardian angel, actually. *Your* guardian angel. No one else can see or hear me." Herbie took a small, gold spiral from his sleeve. "You're my next assignment, Katherine Cassandra." He leafed through several pages. "Looks like we have a lot of work to do, too." Then he smiled, and K.C. gasped to see that all his teeth were solid gold!

K.C. sat back down on the bed. "A real guardian angel?" Herbie nodded. "Come on! I must be dreaming or something." Herbie disappeared from the window, and K.C. felt a hard yank on her ponytail. "Ow!" she yelled.

"See," Herbie grinned. "You're just as awake as I am real." He settled on the bed, close to the open diary.

"Why me?" K.C. asked. "Are you going to save me from being run over by a train or falling down the stairs at school or maybe being kidnapped by jewel thieves? Is that why I need a guardian angel?"

Herbie laughed his windchime laugh. "Put your imagination in neutral, kid. I'm here because of some stuff you've been writing in there." Herbie poked at the diary with his bare toe.

"You read my diary?" K.C. shrieked. "How dare you!"

Herbie sighed. "Look, in my department we don't have to read what people write; we know what they *think*. Take, for instance, the night you wrote this." Herbie made the pages of the diary turn until they came to last Thursday's entry.

DEAR DIARY, GRANDMA'S COMING TO LIVE WITH US. FOREVER! MOM SAYS I HAVE TO LET HER HAVE MY BEDROOM BECAUSE IT'S ON THE FIRST FLOOR AND CLOSE TO THE BATHROOM. IT'S NOT FAIR! AND I HAVE TO MOVE UP TO THE ATTIC. THE ATTIC! FULL

OF SPIDER WEBS AND WHO KNOWS WHAT ELSE. I
HATE GRANDMA FOR THIS! WHY CAN'T SHE JUST STAY
WHERE SHE IS?

K.C. felt her cheeks redden. "I don't really hate
Grandma. It's been real hard for her since Grandpa died."

"I know," Herbie said. "And how about this entry?" He
flipped the diary pages to where K.C. had written several
weeks ago.

DEAR DIARY, I DON'T KNOW WHO I AM ANYMORE!
SOMETIMES I FEEL SO GROWN UP. OTHER TIMES, I
WANT MOM TO TUCK ME IN AND GIVE ME A BEDTIME
HUG. ISN'T THAT WEIRD? MAYBE I'M GOING CRAZY!

"Or how about this one?" Herbie said as the pages
turned.

DEAR DIARY, NONE OF MY CLOTHES FIT RIGHT
AND MY HAIR LOOKS LIKE THE MOP MOM KEEPS ON
THE BACK PORCH! NO WONDER SPIDER NEVER
NOTICES ME. HE JUST THINKS OF ME AS JOSH'S
LITTLE SISTER. I'VE NEVER SEEN ANYONE WITH SO
MANY MUSCLES! EVERY TIME HE LIFTS A BALE OF
HAY HE LOOKS LIKE MR. UNIVERSE. JOSH SAYS
SPIDER IS THE BEST WRESTLER AT THE HIGH
SCHOOL. MAYBE IF I WASN'T SO FLAT CHESTED. . .

K.C. snatched up the diary and closed it. "That's
personal, private stuff!" She fingered the edge of the quilt.
"So what are you supposed to do? Give me a personality
transplant or maybe get me in for plastic surgery?"

"Not quite," Herbie laughed. "The personality and
looks you have will do just fine. I'm here to help you over
some rough spots, to teach you a few survival tricks, to
remind you that God cares about *everything*—from the zit
you're afraid you're getting to the zero you got in math last
week."

K.C. smiled shyly. "You know about that zero in
math?" Herbie nodded. She took the rubber band off her
ponytail and began brushing her hair. "Think it'll work out
all right, Herbie, having Grandma here? She's so old-

fashioned! And what if she embarrasses me in front of my friends?"

"Listen, Katherine Cassandra; there are two things you should know. The first is that things will be all right. The second is that it's going to take work on everyone's part—work, and compromise, and patience."

K.C. looked at Herbie. "And there's one thing *you* should know, Herbie."

"What's that?" he asked, floating in front of her like a helium balloon.

"My name's K.C. Just plain K.C. None of this Katherine Cassandra stuff, okay?"

"Sure thing, kid." Herbie took out his spiral and wrote with a gold pencil: "Prefers to be called K.C."

As K.C. picked up her diary off the bed, she wondered again what it would be like when Grandma moved in. Just thinking about it made her stomach feel funny—like she'd swallowed grasshoppers.

"Don't worry about a thing, kid," Herbie said as he landed on her shoulder. "Things can't get too bad when you've got an angel in your attic!"

* * *

"See, I am sending an angel ahead of you to guard you along the way and to bring you to the place I have prepared. Pay attention to him and listen to what he says."
Exodus 23:20–21

Angel in My Attic   *11*

Day 2

ome on, K.C.! I said I was
sorry!" Martha leaned against the locker next to K.C.'s. Her
arms were full of books, and she was clutching a half-
eaten Snickers bar. K.C. didn't answer. She jerked her
homework out of her locker and banged the door shut
with a loud *whang.* "It's not like I told a lie or something!"
Martha persisted, following K.C. down the hall toward the
waiting buses. Without a word, K.C. climbed aboard Bus 30
just before it pulled out of the school parking lot. "Be that
way then! Who needs you for a friend anyway!" Martha
screamed at the back of the bus, stuffing the last of the
candy bar into her mouth.

K.C. sat on her bed, a crumpled stack of paper beside
her. Sheet by sheet, she was tearing it into tiny pieces.
"What's up, kid?" Herbie asked.
"My temper, Herbie, that's what! I'm tearing up every
note Martha ever wrote to me. What a creep she is!"
"Is this the same Martha who slept over two nights
last week and calls you at least three times every night?"
"Well, if she ever has the nerve to call me again, I'll
sure give her an ear full!" K.C. stopped the ripping and
looked up. "How could she, Herbie?"
Herbie kicked his way through a pile of shredded

paper. "You mean how could she tell Jeff what you said about him?"

K.C. tore the piece she was working on into skinny strips. "I told her not to tell. She promised not to tell! But Jeff walked past me in the hall and said, 'So you think I've got sexy eyes?' Then Jeff and all his friends laughed at me. I wanted to crawl inside my locker and not come out until spring break. I felt like such a fool! If they gave an award for 'Big Mouth of the Year,' Martha would be a real winner. I'm never going to speak to her again as long as I live!"

"She promised not to tell!"

Herbie flew up and sat on the pillow. "As long as you live, huh? That could be a very long time."

"I hope so!"

"That means you'll be looking for a new best friend, right?"

K.C. looked up. "I guess so."

Herbie slid his gold spiral from his sleeve. He licked the end of his tiny pencil. "Let's make a list, then, of the necessary qualities this new friend must possess."

"Well—okay."

"First, she must be intelligent. Right?"

"Someone smart enough to help me with my homework."

Herbie looked up from his writing. "The way Martha helped you with that science project last month?"

K.C. nodded. "And let's find someone who's loyal."

"Right! Someone who'll stick with you even when you get in trouble—the way Martha did that time you had to stay after school and pick up all the trash on the football field because you tossed a gum wrapper out the school bus window."

"She helped me for the whole two hours."

"And let's make her perfect," Herbie said, writing the word in big gold letters. "No mistakes, no slips of the tongue, no—"

"I couldn't stand it, having a perfect friend!" K.C. said. "Then I'd always feel like a real jerk around her."

Herbie looked back over the list. "So you're looking for a best friend who is smart and loyal and makes a mistake once in a while. Don't we know someone like that?" K.C. began folding the rest of the papers she hadn't yet torn. "Look, kid, being friends means more than sharing good times. It means sticking together through bad times, too. It means being able to make mistakes, and knowing your friend will understand and forgive you."

K.C. heard the phone ring downstairs in the family room. "Hey, K.C.," Joshua yelled up. "It's that fat friend of yours—'Marshmallow Martha.'"

"Just you watch your mouth, Josh, or all you'll be able to eat when I get through with you is marshmallows!" K.C. looked back at Herbie and shrugged. "A girl's got to stick up for her friends." Then she hurried down the steps to talk to Martha.

"She sure does, kid," Herbie smiled, as he slid the gold spiral back up the sleeve of his robe.

* * *

If one falls down, his friend can help him up. But pity the man who falls and has no one to help him up!
Ecclesiastes 4:10

Angel in My Attic   15

Day 3

K.C. hurried toward the gymnasium. "I hope it's there!" she said to herself as she ducked into the dark locker room. She smiled when she saw her brush on the bench, just where she had laid it after gym class. As she reached for it, she heard voices coming from the other side of the lockers.

"Did you see what she wore today?" The room echoed with giggles.

"Farmer-in-the-dell time, for sure!" More giggles.

"And her hair—nerd city!"

"What do you expect from someone who reads pork prices instead of fashion magazines?"

"And that cotton flowered underwear! Probably left over from third grade!"

K.C. picked up her brush and started for the door.

"And what kind of name is K.C.?"

"Maybe her parents couldn't spell a real name!"

K.C. felt her knees go weak. They were talking about her! She pressed her cheek against the cold wall of the locker room, fighting back the tears and anger that seemed to swallow her. Then, before the two girls could see her, she opened the door and stepped into the crowded hallway.

K.C. had finished her homework and stood staring at herself in the mirror. She turned sideways, first one way and then the other. She grabbed two pair of clean socks off her dresser and stuffed them inside her sweatshirt. "There, that's better."

"Better than what?" Herbie asked, appearing inside the mirror and smiling his golden grin at K.C.

K.C. blushed and let the socks fall to the floor. "Better than being built like a board," she said. "Herbie, do you think I'm pretty?"

By this time, Herbie had flown across the room and was looking at the color pictures of frogs in K.C.'s biology book. "Of course," he said, without glancing up.

"You have to say that, because you're my guardian angel. You'd probably get your wings taken away if you told me the truth."

Herbie floated over to where K.C. was standing. "And what, exactly, is the truth?"

"I'm ugly," K.C. said. "My hair is ugly, my face is ugly, and my clothes are ugly. Ugly, ugly, ugly! I'm going to spend my entire life in a training bra. I'm a freak. Almost every girl in my class has already gotten her period. But not me! I'm still wearing cotton underwear and waiting!" She plopped down on the bed and buried her head in the pillows.

"Hey, kid," Herbie said, pulling aside the pillow.

"There's nothing wrong with you. You're just growing at a different pace from some of your friends. And you're not ugly. Really. In fact, I think you're beautiful."

K.C. looked up. "What do *you* know! You're not even a real person."

"Thank God!" Herbie said. "But I have known some of the women you mortals consider beautiful."

"Like who?"

"Cleopatra, for one."

"You knew Cleopatra?"

"Of course. *Everyone* knew Cleopatra. She had wealth and power—"

"And beauty?" K.C. interjected, sitting up.

"And beauty, by human standards," Herbie said. "Thick black hair, a fine nose, long lashes that framed eyes as black as starless nights. All Egypt—indeed, all the ancient world—was at her feet. And then there was Delilah."

"You mean Samson's girlfriend?"

"You could call her that. But she was really friend to no one but herself. She was as selfish as she was beautiful." Herbie came close to K.C. "Besides, the kind of beauty Cleopatra and Delilah had wasn't the really important kind."

"What d'you mean?"

"Well, they were only pretty on the outside."

"I'd settle for that!"

"The really important kind of beauty, kid, is the beauty that comes from the inside out. The beauty of kindness and gentleness, of unselfishness and patience. It's the kind of beauty that takes more than exotic eye shadows and trendy hair-dos; it takes work and dedication and a Christ-like attitude."

K.C. walked back to the mirror and looked at herself. "If I'm beautiful on the inside, Herbie, does it show on the outside?"

"Always," Herbie smiled. He poked his toe into the dish of rubber bands on top of K.C.'s dresser. "Why not skip the pony tail and wear your hair down tomorrow?" Herbie suggested.

"It's so straight and stringy!"

"Grandma could help with that."

"Grandma? How?"

"Just grab a handful of cloth out of the rag bag and go find out."

A few minutes later, K.C. sat on the floor, her hair wet from a fresh washing. Grandma sectioned small portions with the end of the comb. K.C. handed up tiny strips of cloth while Grandma tied up each piece of hair. "When I was a girl, this was the only way to get curls. None of those fancy 'lectric rollers and what-not. Wait till tomorrow, child," Grandma laughed. "You'll be so pretty those boys' eyes will bug plum out of their heads!"

"That'll be great, Grams," K.C. said. "But I want to be sure a couple of girls notice, too."

* * *

Your beauty should not come from outward adornment. . . . Instead, it should be that of your inner self, the unfading beauty of a gentle and quiet spirit, which is of great worth in God's sight.
1 Peter 3:3–4

Day 4

In New York we had open campus," Whitney said.

"Open campus?" K.C. asked, sipping her soda.

"We could go anywhere we wanted during lunch. It was cool!" Whitney finished her fries and root beer. "Let's get going. This place is starting to bore me."

The two girls walked toward the library. Whitney walked with a certain sway, with an air of confidence that K.C. admired. Just before they reached the library, Whitney turned down a side street.

"Where you going?" K.C. asked, following her.

From the bottom of her purse Whitney pulled a tiny cigarette.

"I can't handle any more book stuff right now," Whitney said. "I've got to mellow out before we start on that report." Whitney began digging through her purse. "Got a joint on you?" she asked K.C.

At first, K.C. didn't realize what Whitney was talking about. A joint? Then she knew. "Uh—no," she said softly.

Whitney laughed. "That's okay. You can furnish the next one. I've got a stub here somewhere." From the bottom of her purse Whitney pulled a tiny cigarette. She fastened a clip on the end of it and, placing the joint between her teeth, struck a match.

"I, uh—I've got to go," K.C. stammered.

"Don't you want a puff? It's good stuff." Whitney inhaled deeply.

"I—well, I need to get to the library and start on this report."

"Sure," Whitney smiled. "But tomorrow I'm bringing along one for you, too." The smell of marijuana lingered between them as K.C. turned and hurried toward the library.

K.C. knelt in front of the rows of encyclopedias, looking for the volume she needed. Suddenly, the "M" volume slid off the shelf and landed with a thud beside her feet. K.C. looked around. She started to pick up the book, when Herbie appeared on top of it. "This is the one you need, kid," he said.

"No it isn't," she whispered. "I want 'C' for 'Civil War.'"

"Maybe that's what you want, but this is what you *need*." Herbie opened the encyclopedia. "Marijuana," he said pointing at the page.

K.C. looked embarrassed. "You know about that?"

"Of course I know about that!"

"I didn't know what to say, Herbie."

"How about NO?" Herbie suggested.

K.C. sighed. "I had no idea Whitney smoked marijuana. She's just so totally together! The way she dresses, what she says, the way she handles herself with guys. And she's lived in New York. New York, Herbie! I've never even been to Indianapolis except for the state fair." K.C. ran her fingernail along the binding of the encyclopedia. "I should have smoked that joint with her."

"Really?" Herbie said. "And why is that?"

"Because now she probably thinks I'm a real goody-goody—and a hick, besides."

"It's stupid to get involved with drugs."

K.C. looked at Herbie. "If it's so stupid, why does Whitney do it? You just don't want me to have any fun. A little marijuana never hurt anybody!"

Herbie pushed the opened encyclopedia toward K.C. "Read this," he said, as several lines under the "marijuana" entry seemed to light up.

"Marijuana often leads to the use of narcotics or other drugs that produce addiction," K.C. read.

"Listen," Herbie said. "Dope and alcohol are bad news. They hurt your body, kid. And your body is God's special gift to you; it's the temple of his Holy Spirit. Booze and drugs teach you to run away from your problems. You smoke a joint to look cool, chug a can of beer to be popular, pop a pill to feel good—and the first thing you know, you aren't even in control of your life anymore!"

K.C. picked up the encyclopedia and walked back to her table. "But Whitney seems in control of everything, and she smokes!"

"Things aren't always what they seem to be," Herbie said quietly. "Whitney's got problems you never even dreamed of. That's one reason her parents moved here, hoping Hinkle Creek might be a new beginning for her. She's trying to make friends the only way she knows how."

"She won't want me for a friend when she finds out I don't do drugs," K.C. said glumly.

"You might be surprised," Herbie grinned, just as Whitney pulled out the chair across from K.C.

"Mind if I sit here?" she asked shyly. "I could use some help—with my report, and things . . ."

* * *

Do you not know that your body is a temple of the Holy Spirit, who is in you, whom you have received from God? You are not your own; you were bought at a price. Therefore honor God with your body.

1 Corinthians 6:19–20

Day 5

K.C. sat on top of the board fence. She waved to her father as he rounded the corner and started back down the long row. The huge corn picker sputtered and chugged as it sucked in the ripe ears. Taking the note out of her back pocket, K.C. began reading it. Again. Herbie flew up behind her.

DEAR K.C., he read aloud. I TOLD GENE TO ASK YOU IF YOU LIKE ME BUT HE WON'T TELL ME WHAT YOU SAID. DO YOU LIKE ME? I THINK YOU ARE CUTE. WRITE BACK SOON. LOVE, BOB.

"Herbie!" K.C. yelled, holding the note behind her back. "This is confidential stuff!"

"Listen, kid, nothing is confidential stuff to your guardian angel!" Herbie sat on the fence post beside K.C. "So you're in love, huh?"

"I'm not sure I really know what love feels like."

K.C. refolded the note. Her cheeks blushed a little when she looked at Herbie. "I like sitting with him at lunch. And I get these funny knots in my stomach every time he shows up at my locker. But—well, I'm not sure I really know what *love* feels like."

"Funny knots in your stomach, huh? This could be serious, kid. You just might mistake love for a bad case of indigestion!"

"Oh, Herbie!" K.C. laughed. Then she became serious. "Really, Herbie, how will I know when I fall in love? What will it feel like?"

Herbie stood up and brushed at a splinter stuck to his robe. "You humans!" he sighed. "So concerned with feelings and emotions—the thrill of winning a race or passing a test or being kissed for the first time." K.C.'s blush deepened. "But love—real love—is based on facts, too."

"What kind of facts?"

"The kind rock-and-roll songs never talk about," Herbie said. "Love—lasting love—must be based on mutual respect, on shared interests. And true love is unselfish. You don't love someone because he wears a letter jacket and drives a red sports car. You don't love someone because his dad owns a fast-food restaurant and you need a summer job. You love someone for who he is, for what he stands for."

"Oh, Herbie, it all sounds so unromantic!"

"Romance is great, kid. In fact, the Bible is full of it."

"The Bible?" K.C. asked in surprise.

"The Bible," Herbie said. "There's the story of Isaac and Rebekah in Genesis, chapter 24. And a whole book is given to Ruth and her happily-ever-after encounter with Boaz. Jacob and Rachel, Hannah and Elkanah, Abigail and David—God's been authoring romance stories since the beginning of time. When God created human beings male and female, he put in all the special chemistry that makes your palms sweaty and your heart jittery whenever you're certain someone is near. But that's not necessarily love. That's attraction. Of course," Herbie went on, "there's nothing wrong with attraction, either. You need to date, to have fun, to learn how to get along with the opposite sex."

K.C. jumped down from the fence and walked toward the barn. "So how can I know if what I feel is just attraction or really love?"

Herbie flew beside her. "Love demands commitment, kid. It's not an emotion of convenience. Love between two people is a bond, a promise, a fact. What you feel now is the excitement of discovery, the tingle of that chemistry God created in you. Be careful and be smart," Herbie said. "Enjoy dating, but take it slow. You've got plenty of time for the depth and intimacy of real love, the kind of love that marriages and lifetimes together are built on."

K.C. leaned against the barn. Its weathered boards were warm from the afternoon sun. She pulled out the note.

"Don't tell me you're going to read that thing again!" Herbie said, throwing up his hands and shaking his head.

"Only a few more times," K.C. grinned. "Until I'm sure I've memorized every romantic word."

Herbie fluttered his wings. "In that case, you'll have to excuse me," he said as he rose toward the roof, "I've had all the romance I can stand for one day!"

*   *   *

It (love) burns like a blazing fire . . . Many waters cannot quench love; rivers cannot wash it away.

Song of Songs 8:6b–7a

Day 6

oy, how would you like to look like that?" Martha asked, holding out a copy of *Passion Revisited*. On the cover was a girl in a red dress with a plunging neckline. "I bet Spider would notice you then!" Martha laughed as she shoved the book back on the shelf.

"Martha!" K.C. said in a loud whisper, giving her a you-promised-not-to-tell look.

The lady behind the desk cleared her throat, and both girls looked up to see her frown and shake her head "no." Giggling, they ducked behind a shelf of books.

"I've got to find a book on rocks for science," Martha said, popping a Hershey kiss into her mouth and heading for the nonfiction section. "I'll meet you out front in ten minutes."

"Uh-huh," K.C. mumbled, thumbing through the paperback romances on the revolving wire rack.

"Lights out, K.C.!" Mom called from the bottom of the steps. "It's way past your bedtime now."

"Okay, Mom," K.C. called back. She laid the book she was reading on the table beside her bed and clicked off the lamp. Moonlight filled the room. After only a few seconds, K.C. reached under her bed and pulled out a flashlight. Grabbing the book, she buried herself under the covers and began reading. She felt someone tapping her shoulder through the quilt.

"If you're playing hide-and-seek," Herbie's voice sounded hollow and far away, "I think you should know there's no one looking for you."

K.C. turned off the flashlight and threw back the covers. "I've got to finish this book, Herbie! Lady Catherine just found out that the gardener isn't really a gardener and that he's trying to gather evidence against her father for treason!"

Herbie flew over and looked at the cover of the book. "*For Love and Honor*," he read. "Catchy title. Want me to tell you how it ends?"

"No!" K.C. whispered hoarsely. "I want to read it myself."

Herbie poked his toe at the binding on the book. "You checked this out of the public library?"

"Well, sort of," K.C. said.

"I thought your library card was expired."

"It is. I just, sort of, borrowed this book."

"To borrow a book, one needs a library card."

"Look, Herbie, it's no big deal. One book. Who's going to miss it? And I'll return it when I'm finished. Besides, taxes pay for that library and all the books in it—and I'm a taxpayer. Almost. I thought this book looked good so I took it."

"The way your friend Tanya just 'took' those earrings?"

"Lots of kids shoplift," K.C. shrugged. "Besides, Tanya says it's not like stealing from a person. It's just a store. And as much as she spends in there on clothes, they owe her one lousy pair of earrings anyway."

Herbie flew close to K.C. and looked her in the eye. "Do you really believe that?"

K.C. didn't answer for a second. "I guess not."

Herbie flew up and began to pace in the air while he talked. "Stealing is stealing—whether it's shoplifting or taking money out of your mom's purse or copying the answers from someone else's homework or slipping a library book into your backpack without checking it out. The whole idea is to get something for nothing, to help yourself to what's not yours. It's wrong, kid," he said as he stopped pacing and hovered in front of K.C., "and one's as wrong as the other."

"No way, Herbie! How can copying a few homework answers be as bad as stealing a pair of earrings?"

"Every kind of stealing is based on deception. And stealing teaches you to depend on other people to supply you with what you want and need, instead of working for it yourself. But most important of all, stealing is sin."

The room was quiet. K.C. traced the title of the book with her finger.

"Remember the poster hanging in the guidance office at school?" Herbie asked at last.

"The one with all the fish on it?"

Herbie nodded. "It's a picture of a huge fish about to swallow a big fish about to swallow a middle-sized fish about to swallow a little fish."

"Yes," K.C. laughed, "and underneath it says: THERE'S NO SUCH THING AS A FREE LUNCH."

"That's pretty much the way it is, too. You all pay for what shoplifters steal—higher prices on merchandise, salaries for more security guards. Everything has a price tag attached. Stolen books mean that thousands of dollars in taxpayers' money must go for library security systems. But loss of self-respect is the biggest price people pay when they start taking what they haven't worked for or earned."

"Look, Herbie—I was going to return it. Honest!"

"I know, kid," Herbie said as he landed lightly on the bed beside K.C. "But you shouldn't have taken it in the first place—because taking just gets easier and easier."

"I guess so," K.C. said, laying the book and flashlight back on the table. "And tomorrow, first thing, I'll get that book back in the library. No more taking what I'm not entitled to!"

"Good," Herbie said, yawning. "I'm glad we got that settled."

"But tonight," K.C. grinned as she snatched the book and flashlight off the table and scrambled under the covers, "I'm going to find out what happens to Lady Catherine and her mysterious gardener!"

* * *

"Do not steal. Do not lie. Do not deceive one another."
Leviticus 19:11

Day 7

T he important thing, class, is to go through your projects step-by-step. Computers are the tools you'll need for future success. And, remember, a computer is your friend!" Mrs. Martin smiled, but K.C. thought it was a nervous smile. The computer lab at Hinkle Creek was brand new, and everybody seemed a little scared by the gray machines and blinking green letters.

K.C. sat in the back, next to Lisa Harmon. Lisa Harmon was the biggest girl in the class. Not big like Martha was big, from eating too much. But big the way those girls on the covers of magazines were. The boys were always staring at her, but Lisa mostly ignored them. K.C. wondered why. If Jeff were ever to stare at her, she'd be sure to stare back! "She likes older boys," Martha had told her once. "You know, high school stuff." K.C. stared at the blinking cursor on her screen and thought about boys. There was Bob, who had decided it was time for a new girlfriend and sat with Judi at lunch. And there was Jeff, with his sexy eyes. And, of course, Spider. If she had to choose between Spider or Jeff, which would it be?

Suddenly, her cursor began to move across the screen. GREETINGS FROM YOUR FAVORITE HEAVENLY BEING. K.C. glanced over to see if Lisa had noticed. But Lisa's seat was empty. K.C. saw her take the hall pass and leave.

Herbie appeared beside her. "So, how's the computer programming going?"

"Terrible, Herbie," K.C. said, erasing Herbie's message letter by letter. "I can't seem to make my fingers hit the right keys—and my projects never turn out right."

"You've got to follow the manual, kid!" Herbie said, leafing through the pages of the big spiral book on the desk. "Line by line by line."

"I know. But sometimes I get confused."

"Then," Herbie said, walking lightly across the keyboard, "you must remember to use this." He placed his big toe on the HELP key, and the screen filled with words.

"Yeah," K.C. laughed. "I use that key a lot!"

Later that evening, Herbie sat on top of the lamp shade, flossing his teeth with a shiny gold thread. K.C. lay on her bed, drawing stars on the cover of her computer workbook.

"Something on your mind, kid?" Herbie asked as he slid the thread up his sleeve and flew over to the foot of the bed.

K.C. looked up. "I don't know, Herbie. It's just—well, it seems like everybody keeps talking about how important this or that will be for my future. Like computers. The counselor is already talking to us about high-school

Angel in My Attic   33

"What if my future turns out awful? Who knows?"

courses. Mom is pushing college brochures at me. Grandma keeps asking me what I'm going to be when I grow up. And I don't know what I want to do five years from now—or even five *days* from now! It kind of scares me, Herbie. What if my future turns out awful? Maybe I'll end up a bum or something! Or maybe my husband will walk out on me and leave me to raise six kids all by myself! Who knows?"

Herbie stepped onto the cover of the workbook and began tracing with his big toe the outline of the stars K.C. had drawn. "Remember reading in your social studies book how people used to think the world was flat?"

"Yeah. They thought they'd fall off the edge if they sailed too far."

"But Columbus proved them wrong, because he had the courage to test his dream of reaching the east by sailing west." Herbie flew up to look K.C. in the eye. "Unknown things are always scary—that's what makes the future seem so frightening. You don't know what will happen to you five years—or five minutes—from now. But there is Someone who does know how it'll all turn out."

K.C. was quiet for a moment. "God?"

"He knows the end from the beginning," Herbie said, nodding his head. "He sees the whole picture of your life while you can only see the corner called 'today.' "

"But how can I be sure I'm making the right decisions—high school courses and college and marriage and career. Some days I have trouble even deciding where to sit in the cafeteria! What if I mess up the picture, Herbie?"

"Use the common sense and good judgment God gave you, kid. Listen to the adults you trust. Look at what your real abilities and interests are when you begin planning for the future. Don't rush into things. Pray for God's will in your life. And whenever you get uptight about your future, just remember you have a HELP key for that, too." K.C. looked puzzled. Herbie brought her Bible from the bookcase on the other side of the room. "God's Word, kid. It can help you know where to turn; it can remind you of Who's in charge of your future. It can even guide you in making those tough decisions."

K.C. opened her Bible. Herbie turned the pages while she read. When K.C. finally closed the Bible, she laid it next to her bed. "I think I'd better keep this close at hand, Herbie."

"Why?"

"Because," K.C. said, opening her computer workbook to study the keyboard, "I think I'm going to need all the HELP I can get!"

* * *

My help comes from the Lord, the Maker of heaven and earth.
Psalm 121:2

Day 8

I just hope Grandma doesn't come marching through the family room with her teeth out tonight, smiling that gummy grin." K.C. sprinkled the shredded cheese on the pizzas. "This has just got to be the best slumber party ever!"

"Speaking of smiles," Herbie said, eyeing his reflection in the glass door of the oven, "do my teeth look dull to you?"

"Your teeth look fine, Herbie," K.C. said in exasperation. She slid the pizzas in the refrigerator for later. "Maybe Grandma will sleep really sound tonight and not even come out of her room to go to the bathroom."

Herbie flew up to face K.C. "Listen, kid, did it ever occur to you that you might be wrong about this? I mean, maybe your friends would *like* to meet your grandmother."

"Are you kidding? She's too old-fashioned."

K.C. went up to her room while Herbie lingered on the stairway. "We'll see," he smiled. "We'll just see."

"How about you, Judi?" Martha asked in between M&M's. "Have you ever kissed a boy?"

"You mean on the mouth? No, not really. Just on the cheek."

"I kissed a boy on the mouth once," Whitney said. "It was backstage at our school's Christmas play last year."

"What was it like?" K.C. asked.

Whitney shrugged. "I don't know. It was fast, and it was dark. Okay, I guess. Kind of soft and wet."

"I bet Lisa Harmon has kissed plenty of boys on the mouth!" Martha said. The other girls giggled.

"Why do you suppose she's so—you know—big?" Judi asked.

"Vitamins!" Whitney laughed.

"Exercise," Martha said knowingly. "I read it in a magazine when my mother was at the doctor's office last week. You're supposed to do this every night." Martha stood up and began making choppy motions with her arms. "Fifty times every night." The other girls tried it, too. And soon the room was filled with flapping and giggling. They all collapsed back onto the floor.

"I wouldn't want to be like Lisa," Carol said. "All the boys make fun of her just because she's big. And she started her period in fourth grade."

"Fourth grade!" K.C. said, feeling a mixture of awe and anger.

"Let's go around the circle, and you have to tell if you've gotten your period yet," Whitney said. "You first, Martha."

K.C. knew what Martha would say. "No," she said,

Angel in My Attic 37

shaking her head. "Not yet." They went around the circle. Eight no's and only two yes's.

"Let's go around again," Judi said, "and this time you have to tell who the cutest boy in school is. You first, K.C."

Did she mean high school, too? Should she say Jeff or tell them about Spider?

Just then, the door of Grandma's room creaked open. Everyone looked up. K.C. closed her eyes. *Please, God,* she prayed silently, *at least let her have her teeth in!*

At first, Grandma looked surprised to see the family room full of girls; then she looked pleased. Smiling, she came toward them. K.C. breathed a sigh of relief when she saw that Grandma was wearing her false teeth.

"Well, look at all you lovely young ladies!" she said. "And I bet I know what you're talking about—your young men." The girls giggled. "I remember when I was your age. . ." Grandma began.

K.C. felt her throat tighten. *Oh, God, not another boring story!* she pleaded.

"One of my friends said she knew how to find out who we'd marry." Grandma sat down on the couch and pulled her bare feet up under her flannel gown. "She said if you'd take nine licks of salt and then go to sleep without getting a drink, the man you were to marry would come to you in a dream and bring you a drink of water." K.C. looked around the group. Everyone seemed to be interested in what Grandma was saying. "So I spent the night at her house, and we decided to try it."

"Did it work?" Martha asked.

"You bet!" Grandma laughed. "As soon as I fell asleep, a handsome young man came and brought me a drink in a tin cup. His eyes were the blue of the morning glories that grew on my mama's front porch trellis."

"Did you know who he was?" Judi asked.

"I'd never seen him before," Grandma said, leaning forward and looking serious. "But the very next Saturday, when I went to town, I saw him walking down the street. He looked just like he did in my dream!" Grandma laughed. "Next thing you know, he was walkin' me home from church and square dances." She winked at K.C. "That man was your grandpa."

"Wow!" Whitney said. "Suppose it would work for us, too?"

Grandma shrugged as she gathered her flannel gown around her and started down the hall. "You never know!"

"Where's the salt?" Carol laughed as the girls ran giggling into the kitchen.

K.C. watched Grandma close the bedroom door behind her. Herbie appeared on the arm of the couch. "Imagine that," he smiled smugly. "I think the girls actually *liked* her."

"Yeah," K.C. said, "I think so."

"Don't be too quick to judge people, kid," Herbie said. "After all, look how wrong you were about the girls not liking your grandmother."

"Right," K.C. smiled as she started toward the kitchen, "and this is one time I'm glad to be wrong!"

* * *

"Do not judge, or you too will be judged. For in the same way you judge others, you will be judged."
Matthew 7:1–2a

Day 9

"Wally came back to school yesterday," K.C. said as she stood at the end of her driveway, waiting for the school bus. Across the road crows squawked through the stubble of the cornfield, searching for stray kernels.

Herbie was perched on top of the mailbox. "He's been out a long time."

"Ever since his accident. I'd sure hate to have his make-up work!" K.C. laughed. Then she grew serious. "I'd sure hate to have his leg, too. He has to use a cane for a long, long time. The doctors say he can never play sports again. And all because some stupid drunk driver hit him! It's just not fair, Herbie. Why did that have to happen to a nice guy like Wally? Why couldn't it have happened to some creep instead?"

"Life's not like that, kid, with some heavenly referee keeping score, giving goodies to the nice people and throwing bad things at everyone else."

"Why not?" K.C. demanded. "It sounds like a good idea to me."

"Remember that old book your grandmother showed you, the one she learned to read out of when she was a little girl?" K.C. nodded. "One of the rhymes in it says, 'In Adam's fall we sinned all.' When Adam and Eve sinned, way back in the beginning of time, they let evil loose in the world. Ever since then, bad things have been happening. Lots of times they happen to good people."

"But why does God let it be that way? Couldn't he keep trouble away from good people and just zap the evil people with bad things?"

Herbie sat up straighter. "God can, of course, do *anything*. But problems are not punishments God sends because he gets mad at someone. They're the natural results of sin in the world. God's plan is for his people to trust him and live through their dilemmas, not to use him as a 'fairy Godfather' to grant all their wishes and smooth out all the bumps in their lives."

"People who get AIDS just because they had to have a blood transfusion..."

"But it's just not fair—children in poor countries who are starving, people who get AIDS just because they had to have a blood transfusion, old people who get mugged on their way home from the grocery."

Herbie sighed. "No, it's not. That 'fall' Adam took into sin pulled the whole human race in with him. And it turned loose famine and greed and murder and a

Angel in My Attic   41

thousand other ugly things." Herbie shuddered. "Makes me homesick for the place where none of that stuff can ever come, where everyone is happy and healthy—and holy."

"Heaven?" K.C. asked, picking up her book bag as the bus rounded the curve in front of the barn.

"Heaven," Herbie said. "And when the time comes for the score to really be settled, kid, you can be sure that the good people will be rewarded for their lives here on earth. And the bad people—" Herbie frowned. "Let's just say that the place they'll go is so awful it would make every horror film you've ever seen look like a picnic! You'll find things *very* fair in eternity."

"Until then," K.C. said as she walked toward the bus, "I guess I'll just have to put up with the bad things that happen to me, huh, Herbie?"

"Right, kid. Things like that pop quiz you're going to have in first hour!" Herbie called as she boarded the bus.

"Pop quiz?" K.C. groaned as the bus doors closed behind her. "Are you sure?" she mouthed to Herbie out the window.

But Herbie only smiled his golden smile and waved.

* * *

For our light and momentary troubles are achieving for us an eternal glory that far outweighs them all.
2 Corinthians 4:17

Day 10

K.C.'s hand shook as she tried to guide the fabric under the presser foot of her sewing machine.

"No, no!" Mrs. Keithley said, looking over K.C.'s shoulder. "You can sew straighter than that! Rip out that hem and try it again."

K.C. raised the presser foot and reached for her sewing basket sitting on the edge of the cabinet. Scissors clanged and spools of thread rolled across the linoleum as the basket crashed to the floor. K.C. bent down and began gathering stray pins. Mrs. Keithley knelt to help her. "Are you all right?" she asked softly. K.C. felt her eyes filling with tears. She shook her head. "Why don't you go out in the hall for a minute and get a drink?" Mrs. Keithley suggested as K.C. placed her sewing basket back on the counter.

The hall was dark and cool. K.C. pressed her cheek against the cement wall. "You don't look so good, kid," Herbie said from on top of the row of lockers.

"Oh, Herbie," K.C. said, "isn't it awful!"

"You mean about Carol?" Herbie asked as he floated down in front of her.

K.C. nodded. "I'd noticed the bruises on her legs before, but I just thought she—well, bumped into things a lot or something." K.C. took a deep breath. "But when we got dressed for gym today, I saw the spots on her back. At first I thought they were pimples or something—so I kidded her about getting her back in shape before swimsuit season. But she told me—they were cigarette burns, Herbie!"

"I know, kid," Herbie said softly.

"Why would a parent do that to his own child?"

"Then she started crying," K.C. went on, "and telling me how her dad hits her all the time and how he had— had burned her." K.C. walked toward the drinking fountain. "Why, Herbie? Why would a parent do that to his own child?"

Herbie's wings drooped as he talked. "Child abuse is a horrible thing, kid. And it happens over a million times every year. Some parents just can't handle their own problems; they don't know how to deal with the stress they feel so they take it out on their children."

"How can Carol stand it? Why doesn't she run away or tell someone or *something*?"

"Sometimes abused kids come to believe that they

Angel in My Attic   45

must somehow deserve their punishment. They begin to think they're no good. Besides, some are afraid that if they get their parent in trouble, then he really will hurt them." Herbie flew closer. "You know, kid, Carol could use some help."

"But what can *I* do?" K.C. asked as she bent over the drinking fountain.

"She needs a friend," Herbie said. "She needs someone to care about her and to pray for her. That's two things you can do. And you could tell the school nurse."

"I promised Carol I wouldn't tell!" K.C. said, wiping her mouth with the back of her hand. "But. . ."

"But what?"

"But I can't stand to think about Carol and what might happen to her!"

Herbie and K.C. started back toward the home ec. room. "Listen, kid, child abuse is everyone's problem. Most parents want to be helped—they just don't know how to get the counseling and support they need. It's an evil, destructive situation. Hundreds of children every year die at the hands of their own parents!"

K.C. stopped and faced Herbie. "Well, that won't happen to Carol. I'm sure she'd have enough sense to get out before anything like that happened!" They walked on in silence. Then K.C. spoke. "Boy, when Carol has kids, I bet she never hits them or anything."

Herbie sighed. "That's what Carol's father said, too—all the time his father was beating him."

"You mean—"

Herbie nodded. "Carol's father was an abused child, too. It almost always works that way. The abused child grows into an abusive parent. A vicious circle, continued from generation to generation."

"You mean Carol might—someday—"

Herbie shrugged his shoulders.

"What would happen, Herbie, if I told the counselor or someone about Carol? Would she get in trouble?"

"Of course not," Herbie said, his wings perking up just a bit. "A whole team of experts will begin to help her and her family—a psychologist, a doctor, a counselor. I'll even bet your pastor will call on them if you ask him to."

"But I promised Carol I wouldn't tell!" K.C. said. "What about that? Should I break my promise?"

"That depends, kid, on what you think is more important: *not* breaking a promise or breaking a circle of child abuse that can victimize Carol for the rest of her life."

K.C. stepped inside the home economics room door. She took a deep breath and walked up to Mrs. Keithley. "Could I go to the office, please? It's really important."

* * *

Each of you should look not only to your own interests, but also to the interests of others.
Philippians 2:4

Day 11

K.C. reached for her lab coat and safety glasses. "This whole morning's going lousy!" she said to Martha. "I'll probably cut my finger off with a saw or something."

"Shop makes me nervous," Martha said, sliding her wood project off the shelf. "Besides, I always feel guilty when I pass that big pine tree in our front yard, knowing I'm cutting up one of his relatives at school."

"That's stupid!" K.C. laughed.

"So what happened this morning?"

"She grounded me for a week."

"Oh, Mom and I got into it. And she grounded me for a week. No phone calls. Said I needed to learn to control my smart mouth."

Soon the buzz of saws and the whirr of lathes drowned out the girls' voices.

K.C. stood in front of her bedroom mirror, sticking out her tongue—first to the right, then the left, then the middle.

"Okay, kid, I give up," Herbie said as he appeared

perched on top of the mirror. "What are you doing, practicing to be a hummingbird?"

K.C. turned away from the mirror and plopped down on her bed. "Oh, Herbie," she wailed, "how can something so small get me in so much trouble!"

"You mean your tongue?"

K.C. nodded. "Like this morning when I talked back to Mom. Or at lunch today when I told Gretchen I'd never seen anyone wear her hair like that before. I meant it as a compliment! But she got real mad and huffed out of the cafeteria before I could explain."

"And then there was last week," Herbie reminded her, "when Mr. Sowers walked into class late, and you were up front with his glasses on doing a rather unflattering imitation of him."

"Yes," K.C. sighed. "That little bit of comedy cost me two after-school sessions in detention hall."

"You humans have always had trouble taming your tongues!" Herbie said. "James, the brother of Christ, had quite a bit to say about that very thing in his letter to the early church." Herbie flew over to K.C.'s Bible and opened it to the Book of James. "Here," he said, handing her the book, "read chapter 3, verse 2."

"We all stumble in many ways. If anyone is never at

fault in what he says, he is a perfect man, able to keep his whole body in check," K.C. read.

"Remember when you were little and afraid to ride Fleet Foot?"

K.C. laughed. "I thought that horse was the biggest thing I'd ever seen in my life!"

"But your dad showed you how to control her with the bridle, how a tug and pull could make her obey. That little bit in her mouth gave you control over that huge animal. It's the same with your tongue. Learn to control it, and you've got your whole self under control."

"But how can I do that? How can I control my tongue so I won't say the wrong things?"

"Think before you speak," Herbie said. "Imagine how what you say will sound to the other person. And ask God to help you—to make your words kind, to keep your tongue under control when you're tempted to brag or show off." Herbie was quiet for a minute. "You know, kid, when you've really let your tongue get out of hand, there are a few words that can help the situation."

"Like what?"

"Well, if you can make your tongue say it, 'I'm sorry' is usually a good place to start."

"I know," K.C. said as she started downstairs to help with dinner. "I think I'll try that right now with Mom. And tomorrow I'll try it with Gretchen, too."

Later that evening, K.C. was playing a game of trivia with Grandma and Joshua. "You'll never get this one," Josh said, handing her the card with her question on it.

"What is the strongest muscle in the body?" K.C. read aloud. She thought of the pictures she had seen of weightlifters. She thought about how Spider looked when they baled hay. Which muscle would be strongest? Then Herbie caught her attention. He pointed to his mouth and smiled. "The tongue!" K.C. said. "The tongue is the strongest muscle in the body."

"How'd you know that?" Josh asked in surprise.

"Oh," K.C. said, flicking the spinner for her next turn, "I guess you could say I've had first-hand experience with that fact!"

* * *

When words are many, sin is not absent, but he who holds his tongue is wise.
Proverbs 10:19

Day 12

You should have seen Mrs. Martin when she opened her gradebook and that hermit crab wiggled out!" Bob laughed. Everyone else at Gene's party laughed, too.

Martha was busy picking mushrooms off her pizza. "How can people eat these slimy things?"

"I bet you'd eat them if they were covered with chocolate," K.C. said.

"Look at me!" Gene said in a scary voice. "The monster from the bloody pizzeria!" He had smeared pizza sauce on his cheeks and laid two slices of pepperoni over his eyes.

"Gross!" Whitney said. "Is that your idea of fun?"

"You got any better ideas?" Jeff asked.

"Maybe," Whitney smiled, her dimples deep and daring. "We could play spin the bottle."

"All we have is pop cans," Large-Brained Lawrence commented. "Maybe we could play Trivial Pursuit instead."

"Honestly, L.B.," Gene said, taking the pepperoni off his eyes and popping it in his mouth. "Sometimes you're so dense."

Just then Gene's mother came into the family room. "Everyone ready for games?"

"Here it comes, 'pin-the-tail-on-the-donkey time,'" Martha groaned.

But it wasn't "pin-the-tail-on-the-donkey." Instead, it was a game called "Wink-em." The girls all put their chairs in a circle and the boys stood behind them, with their hands behind their backs. One boy stood behind an empty chair. Then he winked at a girl, and she had to jump out of her chair and go sit in front of the winker—before the boy behind her could tag her. Bob winked at K.C. So did Jeff. After a while, the boys and girls switched places. When it was her turn, K.C. winked at Jeff, but Whitney was too fast. Then she winked at Lawrence, who grinned and made a dive for her chair.

When the game was over, Gene brought out cartons of ice cream and lots of different toppings. Martha piled the whipped creme on top of her chocolate sauce. "This is my idea of food—not a mushroom in sight!"

K.C. was sprinkling on nuts when someone bumped her arm. It was Jeff. "So, how about ducking out the back door for a walk or something?"

K.C. felt her hand shake as the nuts spattered on top of her ice cream. "Uh—I don't know."

"There you are, Jeff!" Whitney called. "I was just touching up my lipstick." K.C. looked at Whitney's mouth and, sure enough, she was wearing lipstick.

"I could use some fresh air." Whitney's red lips smiled as she and Jeff went outside.

"Can I get you a Coke?" K.C. looked up to see Large-Brained Lawrence standing beside her, his eyes serious through his smudged glasses.

"Sure," K.C. smiled. "That'd be nice."

"You should never have winked at him," Martha said between bites. "Now he thinks you like him. I can see it now—L.B. loves K.C. forever!"

"Sh-h-h," K.C. whispered. "Here he comes."

It was almost eleven o'clock by the time K.C. got home. She slipped on her favorite T-shirt and climbed in bed without even brushing her teeth. A soft glow appeared on the bottom rail of her bed.

"You asleep, kid?"

"Huh-uh. I'm thinking."

"About the party?"

"Yes, and other things." K.C. raised up on one elbow as Herbie flew up beside her. "Sometimes, Herbie, I hate who I am. I wish I could be as cool with boys as Whitney is. I feel so awkward! And, I know this is terrible to say, but sometimes Martha embarrasses me, even though she is my best friend. She's always eating! And I tried to be nice to L.B. tonight because nobody had winked at him, but now he thinks I want to be his girlfriend."

"It's tough trying to please everybody," Herbie said. "When Jesus was here on earth, he had that problem, too."

"Jesus? You must be kidding!"

"No one has ever been as misunderstood as he was. The disciples wanted him to raise an army and slit the throats of every Roman in Galilee. The Jews wanted him to bow to their interpretation of the law and just be a good, quiet observer. But Christ knew he couldn't please either group. He knew who he was and what his mission was: to die a humiliating death for all sinners, to turn the world upside down with the power of love over hate."

"At least he knew who he was. Sometimes I feel like I don't even know who I am!"

Herbie flew up and looked K.C. in the eye. "You're a first baseman who happens to like perfume and hair ribbons. You're an excellent horsewoman who wants to ride horses, not smell like them." Herbie tipped his halo. "You're a lovely young lady, who behaved just right at the party tonight."

"Really, Herbie?"

"Really," Herbie smiled. "And every day, as you grow and learn, you'll make new discoveries about yourself— what you want and what's important. You'll know who you are."

"It was a cool party," K.C. yawned. "The pizza and the music and the wink-em and—" K.C.'s voice faded.

"Get some sleep, kid," Herbie whispered, pulling the cover over her shoulders. "It takes a while to get used to this party life."

* * *

I praise you because I am fearfully and wonderfully made; your works are wonderful, I know that full well.
Psalm 139:14

Day 13

Mom's going to be so surprised!" K.C. said as she wiped cake batter off the counter top. The oven timer began buzzing. "It's done!" She pulled out the rack. Together she and Herbie looked at the cakes.

"Looks a little raw to me," Herbie said, staring at the gooey mixture.

"Maybe it just needs to be browner. I'll put it down in the broiler."

"I don't know about that, kid."

But before Herbie could say more, K.C. turned the broiler to high and stuck the cakes under it. Within minutes the kitchen was filled with the smell of scorched cake.

"Oh, no!" K.C. grabbed the pot holder and slid the cake pans out. Black smoke rose in little whirls. "They're ruined!" she moaned.

"Maybe not," Herbie said, brushing aside the smoke to take a closer look. "Let them cool and then you can just cut off the burned edges."

After the cakes were cool, K.C. took them out of the pans. She held them gently and scraped the charred edges into the sink. "There, that's not so bad," she said as she set the two chocolate cakes on the counter. But when she

56

looked at them, she realized that one was definitely lopsided. "Now what do I do, Herbie?"

"Humph," Herbie said, examining the cakes. "Looks like a ski slope made of mud."

"This is no time for jokes!"

"Be calm, kid. And make sure you have *lots* of frosting."

K.C. finished beating the icing and brought the big bowl over to where the cakes sat. Herbie grabbed a knife, and together he and K.C. began spreading the top of the lopsided layer with frosting. Herbie talked while they worked. "Your mom will really like this."

"I had no idea baking a birthday cake could be so hard," K.C. said, licking the icing that ran down her thumb.

"Sometimes creating something can be very difficult, especially if the thing you're creating doesn't cooperate."

K.C. looked up. "Are we talking about my cake, Herbie, or something else?"

Herbie smiled. "You catch on fast, kid. Soon you won't even need a guardian angel to tell you things." Herbie cleared his throat and hurried on. "You're God's creation, the very best thing he ever made—better than mountains or constellations or oceans."

"Better than *all* those things, Herbie?"

Angel in My Attic   57

Herbie nodded. "Uh-huh, because you were made in the very image of God himself. And he wants you to be like him, to be perfect. But it doesn't always work out that way."

"That's for sure," K.C. interrupted. She globbed more icing into the low side of the cake. "Seems like I mess up all the time."

"But when that happens," Herbie went on, "God doesn't give up on you. He sticks with you and works to make you all you can be, to make you a creation worthy of your Creator."

Gently K.C. lifted the top layer onto the iced bottom layer and began swiping icing around the sides. Herbie helped by pushing the cake back into place whenever it started hanging over one side or the other. At last the birthday cake was finished.

"So what do you think of my creation?" K.C. asked as she sat at the kitchen table, licking leftover icing from the bowl.

Herbie flew around the cake. Its top was decorated with bright sprinkles and a single candle. "Not bad, kid. It's amazing what a little patience and persistence can do— with all kinds of creations." Herbie flew over and stood on the rim of the bowl. "But there is one thing wrong. Something serious."

K.C. looked up in alarm. "What, Herbie? Did I forget an ingredient? Did I put in salt instead of sugar? What?"

Herbie flew over to the cake. He spread out his arms and said in disgust, "It's devil's food cake, kid—*devil's food*!"

* * *

O Lord, you are our Father . . . we are all the work of your hand.
Isaiah 64:8

Day 14

"Look at this one," K.C. said, holding up a picture of a girl with long, blonde hair. "I could brush my hair a zillion times a night and it still wouldn't shine like that!"

"It's the lights," Martha said, licking her thumb and turning the pages. "These pictures will look great up in your room." She ripped out a page of denim jackets and skirts.

"Girls, girls, girls!" Grandma appeared in the doorway of the kitchen. "What a mess! Paper slivers all over the floor, and all these nice magazines torn to shreds."

"It's to decorate my room," K.C. said. "Mom said it was all right."

"Your mother's just too lenient with you. Now get this mess picked up so I can start peeling potatoes for supper."

K.C. started to say something, but remembered the talk she and Herbie had had about her tongue. Martha began gathering up the magazines. "It's okay, K.C. I've got to get going anyway. See you tomorrow."

K.C. walked Martha to the front porch, then ran up the steps to her room. She slammed the attic door as hard as she could. Even the window panes seemed to wiggle.

"Earthquake season?" Herbie asked, hanging onto his halo.

"I just can't take it anymore, Herbie. Grandma is driving me crazy! All she does is pick on me!"

"It's not as bad as all that," Herbie said, hovering close to the mirror and looking carefully at his teeth. "Do you think these front ones look dull?" he asked as he smiled at K.C.

"Forget your teeth! I need your help."

"Okay, okay," Herbie said, settling on the foot of K.C.'s bed. "What seems to be the problem?"

"Grandma is driving me crazy! All she does is pick on me!"

"Grandma! Grandma's the problem! Yesterday she made me refold all the socks because some of them were inside out. She tells me the same stories over and over. She makes me put on a sweater every time *she* gets cold. Last night when we were doing dinner dishes, she made me dry each prong on all the forks! Just now she had a real fit because Martha and I were cutting out some pictures to hang in my room, and she wanted to start peeling potatoes!"

"She's only trying to help."

"Well, she's not helping. She hemmed my blue skirt and got it so crooked Mom had to do it over after Grandma went to bed."

"Well, her eyesight isn't exactly what it used to be.'

"And I'm so sick of hearing about the 'good old days!' If she tells me one more time about how wonderful things used to be, I'll scream!" K.C. plopped down on her bed and began filing her fingernails.

"It can be tough growing old," Herbie said. "Especially when the whole world seems to be speeding by you. But the worst thing is feeling you're not needed anymore, that you can't really do anything worthwhile."

"Why can't she just watch television or something?"

"The problem with television is that it talks *at* you, but never *to* you. Lots of older people use it for company, but it's a poor excuse for flesh-and-blood conversation." Herbie was silent for a minute. "Grandma watches for your bus every afternoon, waits for you to come bursting in the door full of grumblings or giggles or whatever."

K.C. looked up. "She does?" Herbie nodded. "But she really bugs me sometimes, Herbie."

"I know," Herbie said. "But she loves you—and needs you."

K.C. sighed as she put away the nail file. "I'd never really thought about Grandma *needing* me."

"Loneliness is a pretty awful thing," Herbie said, "and old people are its most common victims. That's one reason your grandma couldn't stand to live alone after your grandfather died. If young people could just give a few minutes—" Herbie looked up to see K.C. grab her new blouse out of the closet and run downstairs. "Hey, where you going?" he called, flying after her.

K.C. sat on the couch beside Grandma. "It's a good thing you brought this blouse down to have me tighten the buttons," Grandma said as K.C. threaded a needle and handed it to her. "In the good old days, things were made to last. Nowadays, it's hurry and get it in the stores.

There's just no pride in workmanship left!" Grandma pulled the needle in and out as she worked on each button. "When I was your age, we made all our clothes, on a treadle sewing machine. None of this fancy electric stuff! Did I tell you about the first Sunday go-to-meeting dress I made all by myself?"

"Tell me again, Grams," K.C. smiled.

And Grandma did.

Herbie, hovering high overhead, whispered to himself, "You're learning fast, kid. Soon you won't need me at all."

* * *

Do to others as you would have them do to you.

Luke 6:31

Day 15

I can't believe the school year is already half over," K.C. said, tossing a forkful of straw into the calf stalls. Her breath came out in frosty little curls.

"I can!" Josh said, cutting the twine off a bale of hay and filling the wooden mangers. "It seems like I've been in school all my life. I can't wait for June. Then just one more year!"

He and K.C. finished the feeding and started toward the house. "I got my new schedule today," she said. "I have Mrs. Cannon for math."

"Old Cannonball's still around?" Josh laughed. "Incredible! She was fossil material when I was at the middle school. Talk about mean! That woman makes junkyard dogs look friendly. And she grades super hard. I still remember that nasal voice of hers." Josh pinched his nose with his fingers and continued in a whiny voice. "Now class, today we will do integers. Sit up. Pay attention. Don't chew gum. Don't talk. Don't *breathe*." Josh let go of his nose and shook his head. "I sure don't envy you, sis."

"Yeah," K.C. said, the frown in her forehead deepening as they went in to wash up for supper.

Later that evening, K.C. stood at the attic window, watching the snow fall. Huge, white flakes floated past her window. "Whenever it used to snow like this, Grandpa

Angel in My Attic   65

would always tell me the angels were having pillow fights," she said.

"That would be a first in heaven!" Herbie laughed.

"Actually, it's just dust falling."

K.C. looked at Herbie. "Dust? Those gorgeous flakes?"

Herbie nodded. "A drop of water in a cloud freezes around a speck of dust. That makes a snow crystal. Then it begins its fall to earth, usually about six miles, changing all the time. When you humans finally see it, that speck of dust has turned into a beautiful flake."

"I remember when I was little and would spend all day making a snowman," K.C. smiled. "How I hated to see the sun melt him a few days later!"

"Nothing lasts forever—not winter, not snowmen. Everything passes. If it's good, like Christmas or summer vacation, it passes. If it's bad, like test days or the flu, it passes. Even semesters don't last forever."

"Not unless you have Mrs. Cannon," K.C. said.

"Not even then."

K.C. walked over to the bed and picked up her schedule. "So what am I supposed to do until this semester with Mrs. Cannon *passes?*"

"Try hard to get along with her. Keep your mouth closed as much as possible. And pray."

"Maybe I could pray that she'd get—I don't know—something that would keep her home in bed for about six months."

"Bad idea."

"Maybe I could pray that I'd get my schedule changed so I wouldn't have Mrs. Cannon."

Herbie shook his head. "No."

"So what *am* I supposed to pray for?"

Herbie paced on the foot of the bed. "Pray for what you need to get you through this semester with Mrs. Cannon!" he said. "All the resources of heaven are available to you humans. God waits to hear from you, to receive your praises and hear your requests. Be specific!

Prayer is more than 'thank you for . . .' and 'please bless. . .' It's a real source of power to help with day-to-day living."

K.C. knelt beside her bed on the big rag rug. *God, it's me. K.C. And I've come to talk to you. I want to tell you that the snow is great! No one else could turn a piece of dust into something so grand. But something besides snow is on my mind. It's Mrs. Cannon. You've probably heard other kids pray about her. She's awful mean! And I'm going to have her every day for a whole semester. I need help, God. Help me keep my mouth shut in class. Help me to listen to the lesson, no matter how boring it seems. Don't let the homework be too hard. Maybe there's some good thing about Mrs. Cannon, something buried deep down under all the mean. If there is, let me see it so that maybe I can like her just a little bit. And most of all, God, let this semester with Mrs. Cannon pass quickly. And let me PASS math, too! Amen.*

* * *

There is a time for everything, and a season for every activity under heaven.
Ecclesiastes 3:1

Day 16

K.C. threw the rock with all her might. It shattered the thin layer of ice and hit the water with a loud *plunk*. Scooping up a handful of pebbles, she hurled them far out into the pond.

"Haven't seen rocks fly like that since David showed that nasty Goliath what God and a slingshot could do," Herbie said, sitting on a low limb of the nearby crab apple tree. "What a great day that was for the troops of Israel! That rock hit Goliath with such force it—"

K.C. turned and walked toward the far side of the pond, kicking at colorless clumps of grass. Herbie flew after her. "Not in the mood for stories?" Herbie asked.

"Oh, Herbie," K.C. said leaning against a fence post. "It's just not fair!"

"What's not fair?"

"If God really loved you, he'd have given you the lead in the school play, right?"

"Today they announced the parts for the play. And I didn't get the part of Elaine. Heather got it instead." K.C. buried her hands deep in her jean pockets. "Heather—who already heads the cheerleader squad and edits the school newspaper and has every boy in school wrapped around her little finger!" K.C. blinked hard, but still a few tears slipped from the corners of her eyes. She began walking toward the house. "I really wanted that lead part in the play, Herbie."

"I know, kid. Jeff got the male lead, didn't he?"

K.C. nodded. "And Heather got him. I saw them leaving together after school, sharing a play book and laughing. It's just not fair! Why does Heather get everything and I'm stuck with nothing?"

"I wouldn't say *nothing*—"

K.C. whirled around and, putting her hands on her hips, faced Herbie. "All my life Sunday school teachers have been telling me how much God loves me."

"He does!"

"And how God can do anything."

"He can!"

"Oh? Well, if God loves me and he can do anything, why is my life such a mess? Why is it I never get the things I want?"

"Let me get this straight," Herbie said, flying in closer. "You think if God really loved you, he'd have given you the lead in the school play, right?"

K.C. stuck out her lip in determination. "Right!"

"Think about that one, kid. It's like saying, 'If my

mother loved me, she'd let me eat Snickers bars for breakfast, chocolate sundaes for lunch, and pizza for dinner every night.' Sometimes you humans don't really know what's best for you. You don't have the ability to see the long-range effects, to determine the real outcome of situations. So someone who loves you—and does have that ability—needs to be in charge. And he is."

"But what would have been so wrong about my getting the lead instead of Heather?"

"Nothing would have been *wrong* with your getting the part," Herbie said as he and K.C. closed the gate behind them and walked up through the back yard. "It just wasn't meant to be. The real issue here, kid, is trust. You've got to trust God with your life, even when you don't get what you want. *Especially* when you don't get what you want. He loves you more than you can know—so much, in fact, that he sent his only Son to die for your sins and make you his child."

"I would've been good in that lead part," K.C. said, shedding her sweatshirt and muddy tennis shoes in the back porch.

"I'm sure you would have." Herbie followed her up the attic steps. "Uh, what part did you get?"

K.C. picked up her play book. "A part that demands talent and organization and a flawless performance." K.C. paused. "I'm in charge of props and lighting."

"Talk about important parts!" Herbie said, waving his hands in the air. "Why, kid, the whole room will light up when you walk in!"

"Oh, Herbie," K.C. laughed, swiping at him with her play book. But with a swirl of light and a tinkle of wind chimes, Herbie disappeared from sight.

* * *

All the days ordained for me were written in your book before one of them came to

70   *Day 16*

be. How precious to me are your
thoughts, O God! How vast is the sum of
them!

Psalm 139:16b-17

Day 17

There, how's that?" K.C. asked, holding up her poster.

"Fine," Mrs. Martin said, placing it with the others. "These will really help promote the Student Council social. It was nice of you all to come this morning and help."

"No problem," Jeff said, capping his marker. "Saturday morning cartoons bore me anyway."

"For sure!" Whitney half-smiled.

K.C. was almost to her bicycle before Whitney caught up with her. "K.C.! K.C.! Wait!" Whitney ran up beside her. "Listen, I told my mom I was going to your house this afternoon."

K.C. looked confused. "Okay, sure. I guess you can come over."

Whitney punched her playfully on the arm. "Silly! I'm not really coming over! Jeff wants to show me this old haunted house down by the river. So we're going to ride our bikes over there and—explore." Whitney laughed. "Should be fun. So if my mom calls your house, tell her I'm in the bathroom or something. Thanks a million! I'll cover for you anytime." Whitney turned and ran back toward the school. K.C. watched her go, then mounted her ten-speed for the long ride home.

"Soui, pig! Soui!" K.C. stood on the bottom rung of the board fence, tossing corn to the pigs. Grunting and squealing, they grabbed for the huge, yellow ears.

"No doubt where the expression 'eats like a hog' comes from," Herbie said, wrinkling his nose at the muddy barnyard gathering. "Pigs seem like such ignorant, greedy creatures."

"They're not as dumb as they look," K.C. laughed, picking up the empty bucket and heading toward the corncrib.

"I didn't tell any lies. I was just doing a friend a favor."

"And some creatures aren't as smart as they look," Herbie said, flying beside her.

K.C. stopped to face him. "And what's that supposed to mean?"

"Look, kid, you know lying is wrong—so the smart thing is not to let yourself be put in a situation where you can be tempted to sin."

"You mean the deal with Whitney? I didn't tell any lies. I was just doing a friend a favor. It's no big deal."

"What would you have said if her mother had called?" K.C. didn't answer. "The Devil is a pretty clever con artist when it comes to making sin look attractive and innocent. But the safest thing to do is just stay away from temptation in the first place!" Opening the door of the corncrib, K.C. tossed the bucket inside. "You know how your grandma's always saying 'Prevention is the best medicine'?" Herbie asked.

K.C. nodded. "She says it every week when she tries to get me to take that yucky castor oil!"

"That castor oil is awful!" Herbie said, shaking his head. "But it's true that prevention *is* the best cure for some things in life."

"Like temptation?"

"Like temptation. Whenever you can, kid, just don't put yourself in a situation where you can be tempted to do wrong, whether it's being alone in the room when tomorrow's science test is sitting on the teacher's desk, or going through your mother's purse when she's not home, or being part of a group that's going to share a six-pack of beer. And it's not too smart to lie for a friend so she can put herself in a bad situation, either."

"Oh, Herbie," K.C. said, stepping into the back porch and pulling off her barn boots, "you make everything sound so easy, like doing right is the most natural thing ever!"

"Well, for some of us it is," Herbie said, straightening his halo. "And for the rest of you—well, it's a struggle. That's why you need to avoid temptation whenever you can. God is always ready to help—but you've got to help yourself, too."

That night, just before bedtime, K.C. knelt on her big rag rug, facing the window. Silver stars glimmered between the tree branches. Bowing her head, she began. *"God? It's K.C. About today—I'm sorry. I'm glad I didn't have to lie* to Whitney's mother. I know I should have told Whitney NO—but, God, she's so cool and quick with words! I really do want to do what's right, but it's so hard sometimes! Help me." K.C. looked up, and the blinking stars seemed to whisper the final words of the Lord's Prayer. "And lead us not into temptation," she prayed, "but deliver us from evil."

From behind her came the soft sound of Herbie's voice. "For yours is the kingdom and the power and the glory forever."

"Amen."

"Amen," Herbie echoed. "Amen!"

* * *

No temptation has seized you except what is common to man. And God is faithful; he will not let you be tempted beyond what you can bear. But when you are tempted, he will also provide a way out so that you can stand up under it.

1 Corinthians 10:13

Day 18

K.C. dropped the pile of fresh laundry on her bed. "Fold the clothes," she said in a whiny voice as she snatched up two white socks. "Feed the pigs, start dinner, stand up straight, do your homework, be good, wash the dishes, practice your piano—" She tossed the clean underwear into her drawer. "Blah, blah, blah, blah!"

Herbie sat in the window, making faces at a blue jay jabbering in the big oak. "You sound worse than he does," Herbie said, nodding toward the bird. Herbie floated over to where K.C. stood brushing her hair.

"Oh yeah? Well, I'd rather be a bird any day! At least he doesn't have two dozen adults telling him what to do every minute of his life!"

"No, but he does have three barn cats circling the tree who think of him as their next meal."

"I'm so sick of adults bossing me around!
Even that moron brother of mine ..."

"Oh, Herbie," K.C. said as she turned from the mirror. "I'm so sick of adults bossing me around! It's always 'Do this,' and 'Do that,' and 'Where are you going?' and 'When will you be back?' Dad and Grandma begin every other sentence with, 'When I was your age . . .' Why won't they just let me live my life, Herbie? I feel like I'm in a glass cage and everyone is looking in, shouting advice every time I turn around!"

Herbie shrugged. "Presidents have advisors; kings have advisors. Even Solomon, the wisest man who ever lived, had counselors. It never hurts to get a second opinion, kid. Everybody needs a little help now and then."

K.C. shook her brush at Herbie. "A little help? We're talking *major* interference here, Herbie. My life's not my own! Teachers tell me what to do all day, and the minute I step in the door from school, Mom and Grandma and Dad pounce on me. Even that moron brother of mine tries to tell me what to do!" K.C. took a deep breath. "What am I, Herbie, hollow-headed or something? Don't they think I know how to do anything without an adult leaning over my shoulder shouting advice?"

"Don't be too hard on them, kid. It's not easy for them to realize just how fast you're growing up. They sometimes forget that you don't need to be told *everything.* Your family and your teachers want you to become a happy, capable adult. They try so hard to help

you because they know that soon you'll be grown-up and become an 'advice-giver' yourself."

"Not me! I'm never going to make some poor kid miserable by trying to run her life!" K.C. began brushing her hair.

"Good for you," Herbie said. "Never tell anyone what to do! Of course if you're a teacher, you might have to make a few suggestions to your class. And if you're a soccer coach, you may need to shape up your team with a few choice words. And if you become a parent—"

K.C. paused with the brush in mid-air, noticing the glimmer of a smile on Herbie's face.

"Most of the things adults say to you now seem like a real pain. But you'll be surprised how much of it will come in handy later."

K.C. laid the brush on her dresser and clicked out the light. "I guess you never know," she shrugged, sliding under the covers.

A soft glow came from the top of the window, and K.C. knew Herbie was smiling. "*You* never know, kid. *I'm* sure of it."

* * *

The way of a fool seems right to him, but a wise man listens to advice.
Proverbs 12:15

Day 19

K.C. laid her social studies book in the top of her book bag. "Boy, that was quite a reading assignment!" she said. "I'll never be able to remember all that stuff for the test on Friday."

Herbie stretched and fluttered his wings. "You've been studying late every night this week."

"Almost the end of the nine weeks," K.C. said, turning down her bed and flicking off the light. "I promised my folks a good report card this time."

Herbie flicked the light back on. "Is that what you told Ryan this afternoon?"

K.C. blinked into the light. "Ryan?"

"Yes," Herbie said, hands on his hips, "Ryan! I heard the two of you talking about the test answers he was going to give you in homeroom tomorrow."

K.C. sighed. "Okay, so Ryan offered me the test answers. He found them on the desk before Mr. Sargent got in the room, and he copied them. All the kids have them! If I don't take them, I'll be the only one who won't get a good grade—and I've studied hard for this exam."

"Look, kid, just because everybody else—"

"Don't give me that same old lecture!" K.C. said. "If the whole class has the test answers, why shouldn't I?"

"Because Christians are different."

"I don't want to be *different*!"

Herbie flew over next to K.C. "Not even if being different means making the world a better place?"

"Come on, Herbie! I'm just one girl in one school in one state in one country; it's a big world! What I do isn't going to make any difference one way or the other."

"He'll think I'm a real weirdo!"

K.C. flipped the light back off and climbed into bed.

"Remember those lightening bugs you used to catch in the summer?" Herbie asked, his wings gleaming from the window sill.

"Sure," K.C. said. "They were like tiny yellow lanterns blinking over the alfalfa fields. I used to put them in a fruit jar and set them by my bed at night, so I could watch them glow."

"And when even one lit up, the darkness in your room seemed to step back a little and make room for the light."

K.C. looked toward Herbie. "So what?"

"So—the world is a very dark place, kid. Sin is strong; if Satan has his way, he'll snuff out every light that tries to shine for what's right. Every good, honest thing you do is like a ray of light. And every ray helps! Besides, look how

Angel in My Attic

brightly those lightening bugs shine when they band together!"

The room was dark and quiet. Finally K.C. spoke. "But what if I fail the test?"

"You've studied hard, kid. And that means you have the right to ask for God's help in getting a decent grade."

"What do I tell Ryan?"

"Just tell him you'd rather take your chances on the test than cheat."

"He'll think I'm a real weirdo!"

"Maybe," Herbie yawned, curling up and folding his wings over him, "but we know it's not true. You're just . . ."

"Different."

"Right!" Herbie said. "In the very best kind of way."

* * *

> ... let your light shine before men, that they may see your good deeds and praise your Father in heaven.
>
> Matthew 5:16

Day 20

I have homework in every stupid subject!" K.C. said, shoving a stack of books into her book bag.

"Me, too," Martha nodded. "Talk about child abuse!" She slammed her locker shut. "I have to hurry. My mom's picking me up for a dentist appointment. I always have about a million cavities! See you tomorrow."

"Bye," K.C. said, using both hands to lift her tote bag.

"Uh—K.C., could I carry your books or something?"

K.C. looked up to see Lawrence standing beside her, his blue hooded sweatshirt making him look incredibly like a Smurf. "No, it's okay," she said, heading for the bus.

"At least let me get the door for you." He stepped in front of her and pushed open the big metal door.

"Thanks," K.C. mumbled, hurrying down the sidewalk.

K.C. threw her books down on the bed. "Homework! Homework! Homework!" she groaned. "Isn't it enough they work us at school for seven hours!"

Herbie perched on top of K.C.'s science book. "Look on the bright side, kid. Lugging all these books home, you'll end up *strong* as well as smart."

"Not funny, Herbie. I'll also be an old lady by the time I get all this stuff done! Math problems to do, a chapter in social studies to read, review questions in science—" K.C. plopped down on the foot of the bed. "I'll never finish."

Herbie was leafing through K.C.'s social studies book, looking at all the colored maps.

"I might as well not even try that math. I never get it right anyway. And what's the use of doing all this English when I always get adverbs and adjectives mixed up? Who cares, anyway? I might as well not even waste my time!" K.C. snapped her pencil in half and threw the pieces across the room.

Herbie looked up. "My, my, my. A little old for temper tantrums, aren't you?"

"What do you know about anything!"

"For one thing," Herbie replied, "I know you *do* care. And I also know that you know how to tackle big jobs."

K.C. looked at Herbie. "And just how do you know that?"

Herbie flew over to K.C.'s dresser and opened the tiny silver music box. Tinkling sounds of "Music Box Dancer" floated around the room. "Remember when you first heard that song?"

"Sure. It was on the radio at Aunt Katie's. I'd never heard such a pretty melody! So I took my allowance and went to the music store to buy the sheet music for it."

Angel in My Attic   *85*

K.C. laughed. "Boy, was it hard! When I took it to Mrs. Brubaker, she told me that the arrangement was too difficult for me, that my fingers were too short to even reach some of the chords."

"But you were determined to play that piece, weren't you?"

K.C. nodded. "Uh-huh. So for months I worked on it, a few measures each week. Then one day, Mrs. Brubaker told me to play the whole piece. And I did!"

Herbie closed the music box. "That's the way it is right now, with your homework. You feel overwhelmed—like you can't possibly do it all. Things in life, too, are piling up on you. Chores, ballgames, Student Council, 4-H, the youth group at church . . ."

K.C. sighed. "I know. I feel like I'm buried by all the things I have to do. Sometimes I just want to shut myself in the corncrib until life gets simpler."

"Life won't get simpler, kid."

"Wow," K.C. said, "you sure know how to cheer a girl up."

Herbie flew over and sat down on the bed next to K.C. "Just handle your homework and chores and activities the same way you handled that tough piano piece."

K.C. was quiet for a moment. "You mean one measure at a time?"

Herbie nodded. "If you try to do everything at once, you'll just be more frustrated. Break down what you need to do into small pieces, pieces you can handle."

K.C. looked at the clutter of books sprawled on her bed. "Measure by measure."

While Herbie rewound the music box, K.C. made a list of each thing she had to do. Soon the room was filled with the sounds of "Music Box Dancer" and the swish of pages as K.C. did her homework—one assignment at a time.

* * *

For there is a proper time and procedure for every matter.
Ecclesiastes 8:6

Day 21

"Which North American mountain range has the highest peak?" Mr. Sargent's eyes scanned the room. "K.C.?" At first K.C. didn't hear him. She was busy writing a note to Gene. "K.C.!" he said louder.

Suddenly K.C. looked up. Mr. Sargent was standing over her, his face red and frowning. "Uh—," she muttered. "I didn't hear the question."

"No wonder!" he smirked, jerking the note off her desk. "Looks like you were busy doing something really important—like writing to your boyfriend."

"He's not my boyfriend!" K.C. protested.

"I'm not going to waste precious class time reading this aloud," Mr. Sargent said, taking a thumb tack from his top desk drawer. "I'll just post it here for everyone to read." He stuck the note in the middle of the huge bulletin board. "And now, K.C., perhaps you'd be so kind as to direct your attention to the mountain ranges of North America. Turn to page 235 and read the first paragraph aloud."

Muffled giggles mixed with the swishing of pages as K.C. opened her geography book and began to read.

DEAR DIARY, K.C. wrote. THIS HAS BEEN THE WORST DAY OF MY LIFE.

"Let's see," Herbie said, reading over her shoulder. "That makes three 'worst days of your life' this week."

"I mean it this time!" K.C. said. "Couldn't you zap me up to heaven so I never have to go back to school again?"

"Sorry, kid, but 'zapping' you up to heaven isn't exactly on today's schedule."

"I've never been so embarrassed in my life!"

"You mean the note?"

"I mean the whole day!" K.C. yelled, throwing out her arms and shaking her fists. "On the bus this morning, Josh started yelling from the back seat things he'd read in my diary. And when I got up to slug him, the bus driver screamed at me to sit down or she'd report me to the assistant principal. Then, when I went to the library to get a book, I pulled out this one that looked really good—and the whole shelf came tumbling down around me. Everyone in the room clapped."

"And then came the note?" Herbie asked.

"And then came the note," K.C. sighed. "I kept wishing the floor would open up and swallow me. It was just a stupid note about the track meet after school. But by now the whole school has probably read it! Wait till

Angel in My Attic   89

tomorrow when Gene finds out! What a jerk he'll think I am."

"You're right," Herbie said.

"About being a jerk?" K.C. asked in surprise.

"No," Herbie said, "about this being the worst day of your life. So far."

"What d'you mean, 'so far'?"

"Just that being embarrassed, making mistakes, and feeling dumb is part of life. It's not going to go away, like measles or a bad cold."

"Doesn't it ever get better, Herbie? Josh seems to have life pretty much under control."

Herbie laughed. "Josh has just learned how to handle some things—and you will, too. It's part of growing up, of learning that something is 'worst' only because you don't have many things to compare it to. Live a while, kid, and today won't seem so bad."

"What about tomorrow, when Gene finds out?"

Herbie shrugged. "He's not going to be thrilled, but it won't exactly classify as one of the great disasters of the world, either."

K.C. looked at her diary entry: DEAR DIARY, THIS HAS BEEN THE WORST DAY OF MY LIFE! She picked up her pen and added, AT LEAST UNTIL TOMORROW!

* * *

Therefore do not worry about tomorrow, for tomorrow will worry about itself. Each day has enough trouble of its own.

Matthew 6:34

Day 22

"By the way," Mom said as she rinsed the last of the dishes, "Janice is coming over to spend the weekend."

K.C. almost dropped the plate she was drying. "Janice? Here?"

"That's right. I saw her mother in the supermarket this morning. Seems they needed to be away for a few days but didn't want to leave Janice alone. So I invited her over here. Isn't that nice?"

K.C. felt like she was going to throw up. "Nice."

"I knew you'd be pleased," Mom beamed. "You two have become such good friends since they moved here last month."

K.C. swiped the cloth across the dishes as fast as she could, shoved them in the cabinet, and then ran up to her room to find Herbie.

"Herbie. Herbie!" Silence. "Come on, Herbie! I need you!" K.C. yelled.

"What's all the commotion about?" Herbie said, flying in the door with his toothbrush in his hand. "I was just buffing the shine on my teeth."

"Forget about your teeth, Herbie. We've got real problems."

"Such as?" Herbie asked, sliding the toothbrush up his sleeve and sitting crosslegged on K.C.'s pillow.

"Janice is coming over to spend the weekend."

"Is this the same Janice you've been talking about for weeks, the one who invited you to her skating party?"

K.C. nodded.

"So what's the problem?" Herbie asked.

"She can't come over here!" K.C. said, wringing her hands and pacing back and forth. "Maybe I could get sick—really sick." She turned to Herbie. "Could you get me a germ from somewhere? Nothing serious, like malaria. Just something contagious enough to make me too sick for company."

"I most certainly will not!" Herbie huffed. "How would that look on my report: 'Infected human with germ so she would get sick.'" Herbie stood up and put his hands on his hips. "*Why* can't Janice come over here?"

K.C. sighed. "Because—well, I kind of exaggerated. I told her my father was a land baron who owned a thousand acres and that we had a big house with an in-ground pool and TV sets in every room!"

"*Kind of* exaggerated!" Herbie shook his head in disbelief.

"Well, I wanted her to like me!" K.C. wailed. "And she said they had six bedrooms and a live-in maid. I didn't want her to know that my father could barely make ends

Angel in My Attic   93

meet on the farm and that my house was so old and small I had to have a bedroom in the attic. Oh, Herbie, I just *can't* let her come here!" K.C. bit her lip to keep from crying.

"It seems to me the real problem is not that Janice is coming here. The real problem, kid, is that you made up such wild stories in the first place." Herbie flew down to where K.C. sat on the big, rag rug. "Pride, kid. That's what made you lie about your family and your house. Wanting to be something you're not, pretending to have more than you do. The important thing is not what you have or where you live; it's who you are." Herbie straightened his halo and flashed his brightest smile. "And you, Katherine Cassandra, are a truly terrific human being."

"I just hope Janice thinks so after she sees where I really live!"

Janice and K.C. had finished the dinner dishes and lay stretched out on the attic floor, playing Monopoly. "You have such a neat room!" Janice said as she moved her piece to PARK PLACE. "It's like having your own apartment almost, being up here by yourself."

"I guess so," K.C. shrugged.

"I have to share a room with my little sister, and she's always breaking my things or whining for me to play with her."

K.C. looked up from the board. "I thought your house had six bedrooms."

Janice hesitated. "Guess I exaggerated a little. I just wanted you to like me."

"Well," K.C. smiled. "I know how that is. But I like you for who you are, not what you have."

"Thanks, I like you too," Janice smiled back. "But right now I hope you have $200. You landed on my property!"

* * *

"Watch out! Be on your guard against all kinds of greed; a man's life does not consist in the abundance of his possessions."

Luke 12:15

Day 23

"Then the prince took the princess in his arms and kissed her. And they lived happily ever after," K.C. read.

"Tell me another story!" Meg said.

"No more stories tonight," K.C. laughed. "It's time to go to sleep now. Good night," K.C. said, kissing Meg lightly on the forehead.

"Leave on a light!" Meg said.

"I will." K.C. flicked on the tiny dresser light before she clicked off the overhead bulb. "Now you go to sleep."

Back in the family room, K.C. began picking up the toys she and Meg had played with. "So, how's the babysitting?" Herbie appeared behind the wheel of a red toy sports car.

"Fine," K.C. said. "It's always fun to watch Meg. All we do is play until time for her to go to bed." K.C. opened the lid to the big toy box and began putting things inside. "I had a truck just like this one," she smiled. One by one, K.C. placed the toys in the box. "You know, Herbie, when I was little, I couldn't wait to grow up. But now, sometimes . . ."

"Sometimes what, kid?" Herbie asked, flying over and perching on top of the toy box lid.

"Well, sometimes I miss being a little kid. Isn't that weird?" K.C. held a doll in her hand. "I remember rainy

Saturdays when Martha and I would play dolls all day. We'd pretend they were us, always going off on dates with handsome boys or discovering a new continent or saving the world from some awful aliens." K.C. laughed. "And somehow I thought growing up would be like that—always exciting and always fun."

"But it's not, is it?"

K.C. shook her head. "No, sometimes it's a little scary."

"By the time you humans realize how much fun it is to be children," Herbie said, "you're adolescents—with new responsibilities, new freedoms, and new fears."

"That's for sure!" K.C. said as she laid the doll in the toy box. "The only thing I used to be afraid of was some imaginary monster I thought lived in my closet. Now I'm afraid that I don't look right or that what I say will sound stupid. I'm afraid I'll wake up one morning and my face will be one giant pimple. I'm afraid I'll spend my whole life in a training bra. I'm afraid I'll get fat, and I'm afraid I'll be the very last girl in my whole class to get her period." She stacked the books she and Meg had been reading. "In fairy tales everyone always lived 'happily ever after.'"

"Yes," Herbie smiled, "Cinderella never had a zit in her life, and Snow White never once worried about bad breath.

Angel in My Attic

But in real life, it's not like that. You're changing, kid. The little girl who used to play with dolls is now the young lady who helps with housework and struggles with homework, who'd give anything to figure out how to get Spider to notice her and L.B. to leave her alone. You're turning your back on the world of childhood and facing the frightening—but exciting—world of adulthood. And some days, when you look back into that childhood world, it's only natural to wish you could return."

"Things were just so simple then! No pressures— except Mom telling me to practice my piano. Now my friends pressure me to cheat on tests or smoke marijuana—or wear jeans with just the right labels. My teachers pressure me for perfect homework and a 'better attitude'! Even my folks always seem to be pushing me. Nothing's like it used to be!"

"Some things are," Herbie said.

"Name one."

"In Sunday school you learned the Bible verse: 'God is love.' It was true then, and it's still true now. God loved you when you were a dimpled three-year-old, and he loves you now— with all your fears and problems and potential. He knows what you're going through—even better than you do. And he wants to help you, if you'll just let him."

K.C. was about to close the toy box when she saw the game. "Oh, look Herbie, Candyland! I haven't played this since ..."

"Since you were in first grade," Herbie finished.

K.C. traced with her finger the outline of lollipops and candy canes on the game's lid. "Hey, Herbie," she said, smiling. "Do you think maybe the two of us could play?"

"Why not?" Herbie said, his tinkling laughter filling the room. "I always was a *sucker* for a good time!"

* * *

When I was a child, I talked like a child, I thought like a child, I reasoned like a child. When I became a man, I put childish ways behind me.

1 Corinthians 13:11

Day 24

ﾠ

And I guess it was a pretty good book, if you like dog stories," Gene said, starting toward his seat while he was still speaking.

K.C. tried to swallow, but a knot the size of New Jersey blocked her throat. Mrs. Martin fingered the index cards with their names and the titles of the books they'd read. K.C. squeezed her eyes closed. *"Please, God, don't let her pick me!"*

"Well," Mrs. Martin said, "we only have five people left. I think we'll save them for tomorrow. Use the rest of the period to study your vocabulary."

Out in the hall, K.C. and Martha headed for science. "Want an M&M?" Martha asked, holding out a handful of colorful candy.

K.C. shook her head. "No thanks. I couldn't eat a thing. My stomach feels full of yellowjackets. I hate oral book reports! I feel like such a fool standing up there 'uh-ing' and 'umm-ing' and stuttering like Porky Pig."

"Everybody hates them," Martha said, popping the candy into her mouth. "But it's just something you live through, like trips to the dentist and hugs from relatives you hardly know."

The school bus bounced over chuckholes in the gravel road. K.C. sat alone in the back seat, looking out the window at passing mailboxes and silos.

"I've been on oxcarts that ride smoother than this thing!" Herbie said, hanging onto his halo as the bus hit another bump. K.C. didn't answer. She just stared out the window and fingered the edges of her library book. "What's the matter, kid?"

"It's those dumb oral book reports in English. I can't do it, Herbie! And tomorrow I'm going to get an F."

"You read the book, didn't you?"

"From cover to cover."

"So why can't you give the report?"

"Every time I try to get up in front of the class, my face turns redder than a tomato patch in summer. I forget everything I wanted to say. I just can't do it, Herbie. And Mrs. Martin can't make me! As soon as I'm old enough to be on my own, I'm going to get away from people like her who just want to embarrass me."

The bus stopped with a jerk at the end of K.C.'s driveway. She and Herbie got off and started toward the house. "As hard as this may be for you to believe, Mrs. Martin is not out to get you. The reason she wants you to give that oral book report is not to embarrass you in front of your friends or to make your life miserable."

"So why *is* she doing it?"

"She's trying to teach you the most important skill you may ever learn—communication. Half of the troubles you humans have is because you can't communicate with each other! People talk without thinking, hear without listening. Mrs. Martin wants to teach you to organize your thoughts, to say what you mean."

K.C. leaned against the back of the house. "But I can't do it, Herbie. I can't! I feel like everyone is waiting for me to mess up so they can laugh at me."

"Remember the first time you had to climb the rope in gym, the big one with knots, that hangs from the ceiling?"

K.C. nodded. "I was scared to death. I kept going to

the end of the line, hoping the bell would ring before my turn came."

"And how do you feel about that rope now?" Herbie asked.

"It's just about my favorite thing in gym," K.C. smiled. "I can climb faster than some of the boys, even."

Herbie fluttered in front of K.C. "The way to overcome fear, kid, is to face it. David defeated Goliath because he took those first few steps toward him. Joshua conquered the Promised Land because he advanced instead of retreated. Moses overcame Pharaoh because he met him head-on. You learned to climb that rope because you put one hand over the other and *tried*."

"But giving an oral book report is different, Herbie!"

"It's different—and it's the same. There'll always be challenges that scare you, and there'll always be a God who waits to help you with those challenges."

K.C. started in the back door. "Well, I guess I can *try*," she said. "And at least I can't get any points taken off for spelling!"

* * *

I can do everything through him who gives me strength.
Philippians 4:13

Day 25

But why, Mom? Why can't I go?" K.C. asked.

"We've been over this before," Mother said as she pushed the rolling pin across the pie dough. "You're too young to just roam the mall by yourself for hours and hours."

"I won't be by myself!" K.C. wailed. "Martha will be with me. And it's only for three hours."

Mother wiped her hands on her apron. "No, K.C. That's final. I don't want to see your picture end up on a missing child poster somewhere."

K.C. stormed out the back door before her mother could finish. She walked to the end of the yard and leaned against the big maple tree. Herbie lay on a low branch, his head propped up with one elbow. "Sounds like 'Home Sweet Home' isn't quite so sweet today," he remarked.

"She treats me like such a baby!" K.C. yelled. "I don't want to see you end up on a missing child poster," K.C. said in a high voice, imitating her mother. "Why can't she realize, Herbie, that I'm not a child anymore?" K.C. sat down on top of the picnic table.

Grandma came walking up through the yard, stopping now and then to admire the tulip blooms. When she saw K.C., she came toward her. "March winds and April showers, all help to bring May flowers," Grandma smiled.

"Sure," K.C. mumbled.

Grandma came closer. "What's the matter, child?"

"Don't call me child!" K.C. said. "I'm not a child; I'm a young lady."

Grandma chuckled. "That you are, darling. But to me even your mama's a child. Seems like no matter how old they get, your children always seem like just that—children!" As she started for the house, Grandma turned back and waved to K.C. "Good day, *young lady*," she laughed.

K.C. watched her grandmother open the back door and disappear inside. "Is it true, Herbie? Will Mom always think of me as a child? Won't she ever let me grow up?"

Herbie floated down and stood on the picnic table. "Of course she'll let you grow up; she has no choice about that! But you'll always be her child, and she'll always love and try to protect you."

"I don't want to see your picture on a missing child poster somewhere."

"Can't you do something to make her see that I'm almost grown up *now*, something to make her stop treating me like a baby?"

Herbie scratched his head through his halo and thought. "No, there's not much I can do to convince her. But there are a few things *you* can do."

"Anything!"

"You could show her how mature you are—by accepting responsibility without complaining, by doing your chores without being reminded, by getting along with Josh, by not always having to have your own way—"

"Okay, okay!" K.C. said. "I get the idea." She started toward the house. "But how can I call Martha and tell her my mom won't let me go to the mall without a chaperon? No one wants a baby for a best friend!"

"Having a mother who cares about you doesn't make you a baby," Herbie said. "It makes you lucky."

"That's easy for you to say! You don't have to tell Martha the bad news."

Just as K.C. opened the back door, the phone rang. "I'll get it," she yelled. K.C. picked up the extension in the kitchen. "Hello?"

"Hi, K.C. It's me, Martha. I just called to tell you—well, I can't go to the mall like we planned."

"Really?" K.C. asked. "Why not?"

Martha sighed. "You're never going to believe this," she began, "but my mom had a fit when I told her what we wanted to do."

K.C. laughed. "I can believe it, Martha. Boy, can I believe it!"

* * *

Children, obey your parents in the Lord, for this is right. Honor your father and mother.

Ephesians 6:1–2a

Day 26

It seemed to be the only thing anybody was talking about at school that morning. "Did you hear?" Martha asked K.C. as soon as she got to her locker. "Marcie killed herself last night!"

K.C. felt the numb feeling deepen. "Yes, I heard it on the bus."

Between every class, K.C. could hear the comments in the hallway.

"I heard she had an awful fight with her mom and dad over those wild clothes she wears—I mean, *wore*."

"They found her in the closet. She'd hung herself with one of her belts!"

"When she didn't come down for dinner, her mom sent her little brother up to check."

K.C. dropped her unopened lunch sack into the trash bin at the end of the sidewalk. "Not hungry, kid?" Herbie asked.

K.C. shook her head. "All I can think about is Marcie. Yesterday she ate lunch right across the table from me and today she's—she's dead."

Herbie flew up and sat on K.C.'s shoulder. He wiped a tear from the corner of her eye.

"When Grandpa died, it was awful—but he was old and sick. Marcie was so pretty," K.C. went on, her voice starting to break. "Why would she kill herself?"

Herbie sighed. "Life is so precious, yet some humans let it go so easily. Sometimes people kill themselves to hurt those closest to them, as a way to get even for not getting their own way. Sometimes people feel so desperate and alone that they don't want to face another day. Sometimes a person only means to scare the people who love him into paying more attention to him by *almost* killing himself—but ends up really dying. Whatever the reason, suicide is a senseless, stupid waste."

"I used to envy her," K.C. said quietly. "She always looked—just right. Even her teeth were perfect!"

"And while she was smiling that perfect smile," Herbie said, "she was hurting inside, crying where no one could see the tears."

"I guess you never really know how someone feels, do you?"

"Yesterday she ate lunch right across the table from me and today she's ... dead."

"Everybody hurts," Herbie said. "Some people just show it more. Some handle their hurts by acting tough, others by finding a friend to confide in. No one's life is as perfect as it seems. And everyone needs someone to talk to, someone to help him or her make sense of the crazy things that happen."

K.C. smiled. "Someone like a guardian angel, maybe?"

Herbie stood up straighter. "Guardian angels are, of course, excellent sources of help. But I was thinking of Someone even higher up."

"God?"

Herbie nodded. "He's the one who's always available to listen—and help. No problem's too big, or too small."

The bell blared the end of lunch. "I miss her, Herbie," K.C. said as she walked toward the building.

"When someone dies, it's as though a hole opens up—a hole made of cold sadness."

"What happens to the hole, Herbie?"

"Eventually, slowly, it fills up—with time and memories."

"Uh-huh," K.C. said as she pulled open the school door, "that's the way it is with Grandpa. It still hurts when I think of him, but in a different way than it did at first." K.C. grabbed her books from her locker and headed for class.

"See you later, kid," Herbie said, hovering behind her.

"Aren't you coming to choir with me? We're practicing for our spring concert."

"Ah—no," Herbie said, fingering the edges of his robe. "All that singing makes me a little homesick for some heavenly harmony."

With a sigh, Herbie disappeared from sight. But for just a moment, a perfectly pitched "Hallelujah" lingered in the empty hallway.

* * *

Praise be to the God and Father of our Lord Jesus Christ, the Father of compassion and the God of all comfort, who

comforts us in all our troubles, so that we can comfort those in any trouble with the comfort we ourselves have received from God.

2 Corinthians 1:3-4

Day 27

he smell of disinfectant burned K.C.'s nose. She dipped the rag into the bucket of water and began wiping the fronts of the lockers. Bright lipstick smears disappeared as she worked.

"How's it going, kid?" Herbie asked.

DEAR DIARY, I WILL HATE MRS. HOPSON FOREVER. MAYBE LONGER.

"Oh, swell, Herbie." K.C. kicked the bucket out of her way. Brown, soapy water splashed onto the cement floor. "Washing down this stinking locker room was exactly the way I wanted to spend my lunch hour." She took the spray cleaner and began working on the window between Mrs. Hopson's office and the locker area. In bright red lipstick was written: GYM STINKS AND SO DOES THE TEACHER. One by one the letters vanished. When the window was clean, K.C. sat down on the bench to rest. "You know what really makes me mad about this whole thing, Herbie? It's being blamed for something I didn't do. Mrs. Hopson wouldn't even listen to me when I tried to tell her I didn't know anything about what happened to her precious locker room! She just kept waving those mushed-up tubes of lipstick in my face and saying, 'I found these in your locker. I found these in your locker.' Big deal! I suppose it never occurred to her that someone mean enough to write all over her locker room with lipstick would also be mean enough to throw the used tubes into some innocent person's locker. Mine, for instance." K.C. dumped the dirty water down the drain just as the bell rang for the end of lunch.

K.C. opened her diary and began writing. DEAR DIARY, I WILL HATE MRS. HOPSON FOREVER. MAYBE LONGER.

"Sounds like you plan on holding a grudge," Herbie said, underlining the FOREVER with a swirl of light.

"Why shouldn't I?" K.C. demanded. "I didn't even do anything, and she made me wash every stupid lipstick mark in sight!"

"Grudges get pretty heavy to carry, kid."

"You don't know what it's like to be punished for something you didn't do!"

"You're right. I don't. But God does."

"God?"

"That's exactly what happened when he came to earth in the form of a man. Even while he was busy teaching

Angel in My Attic   *113*

and healing people, Christ's enemies accused him of being a drunkard and a sinner. When he was only thirty-three, he died the cruel death of the cross. The only perfect man to walk this earth suffered the pain and humiliation of a criminal's death so that mankind might be free from the slavery of sin. His innocence was complete. So was his sacrifice. He gave himself willingly into the unjust hands of his accusers, knowing it was the only way to bring sinners back to God. And even in his final moments of agony on the cross, he chose the alternative to grudge-bearing."

"What alternative?" K.C. asked softly.

"Forgiveness," Herbie said. "Letting go of the hurt injustices cause."

"So you're telling me I have to forgive Mrs. Hopson?"

"I'm just telling you this. The world is full of people who make mistakes—and you can't go around hating everyone who hurts you. If you do, you'll soon forget how to love."

K.C. looked at her diary entry. "It wasn't fair, Herbie."

"I know, kid."

"And I'm not sure I can forgive her."

"Just give it a try," Herbie smiled. "Forgiveness can feel pretty good."

K.C. picked up her pencil and wrote. MAYBE I WON'T HATE HER FOREVER—BUT AT LEAST UNTIL MY HANDS STOP SMELLING LIKE DISINFECTANT!

* * *

Be kind and compassionate to one another, forgiving each other, just as in Christ God forgave you.
Ephesians 4:32

Day 28

What do you mean you're moving?" K.C. asked.

Martha poked her straw deep into her milkshake. "We're just moving, that's all. My dad's company wants him to start up a new office and so we're moving."

"That's thousands of miles away! I'll never see you again!"

"But California!" K.C. gasped. "That's thousands of miles away! I'll never see you again!"

"Don't say that, K.C. I can't stand it if you say that. Of course we'll see each other! You can fly out. And in just a few years we'll have our licenses." Martha gave her straw a loud *slurp*. "Mom and Dad have been fighting a lot lately. Maybe the move will help. But I can't stand the thought of a new school and no friends and—"

"Let's get out of here," K.C. said, tossing her paper cup into the trash can.

The girls walked toward the library. "Remember when we first met?" Martha asked.

K.C. nodded. "Ballet lessons. First grade."

"The ballet didn't last." Martha's laugh was soft and sad. "But the friendship did, didn't it?"

K.C. held open the library door for Martha. "Yes, it sure did."

"I can't believe Martha's moving!" K.C. said, tossing her books on the kitchen table. She poured a glass of juice and stood looking out the kitchen window at the rusting swing set. "The hours we spent out there! And now she's moving." K.C. whirled around to face Herbie, who was sitting on the edge of the kitchen table, his legs dangling over the side. "I hate good-byes."

"I know what you mean, kid."

"I'm never going to be best friends with anybody again!"

"Why not?" Herbie asked.

"Because every time I really care about someone, something like this happens. First it was Poco. I loved that big barn cat! Carried him around with me like a doll. Then one day he just disappeared. I looked everywhere, but he was gone." K.C.'s voice tightened. "And then there was Grandpa. He was my very, very best friend. He would always buy me gumdrops and take me fishing and make

Angel in My Attic   117

me feel so grown-up, so important. Then he died. And now Martha's deserting me, too!"

"Hold on, kid!" Herbie said, flying over and standing on the kitchen counter. "No one's deserting you. Barn cats come and go; human beings die; people relocate. You'll find another best friend."

"No! Why should I? I can't count on anyone to stick around for long. No one!"

"There is *someone* you can depend on. Someone who'll never leave you."

"You mean you, don't you? That's sweet, Herbie. It's nice to know that you'll always—"

Herbie shifted his feet nervously. "No, no, kid! I, uh—I wasn't talking about me."

K.C. looked surprised. "Then who?"

"I was talking about the Holy Spirit."

"Holy Spirit?"

"When Christ came back to heaven after his resurrection, he sent him into the world. The Holy Spirit lives inside every Christian, a constant reminder of God's presence and love."

"How can I know he's there?"

"The Holy Spirit is a sort of conscience, that small voice you hear warning you not to give into temptation. And he's a comforter, too—that warm, calm feeling you have when you turn to God with your problems and failures."

K.C. picked up her books. "Can I ever see the Holy Spirit?"

Herbie shook his head. "He's a *spirit*, part of God. But you can feel him, if you believe with all your heart."

"I'm really going to miss Martha," K.C. said, starting toward her room. "I'm sure glad I'll always have the Holy Spirit and you."

"Uh, kid," Herbie stuttered. "About your always having me. Well, there are other kids—"

"K.C.!" Mother called from the back door. "Come help me carry in the groceries."

"Coming!" K.C. said, laying her books on the bottom of the attic steps. "We'll have to talk later," she called over her shoulder to Herbie.

"Sure thing, kid," Herbie sighed, watching K.C. run down the walk. "We'll have to talk later."

* * *

"And I (Jesus) will ask the Father, and he will give you another Counselor to be with you forever—the Spirit of truth. The world cannot accept him, because it neither sees him nor knows him. But you know him, for he lives with you and will be in you."

John 14:16–17

Day
29

K.C. lay on the rug, an open pack of markers beside her. "Should I make the letters blue or red?" K.C. asked.

"Both," Herbie said.

K.C. began coloring. "I wish doing this biology project had been as much fun as drawing the cover is."

"At least you got to work with a partner."

"Yeah, that helped."

Herbie smiled. "Especially since yours just happened to be Large-Brained Lawrence, the smartest boy in class."

K.C. grinned. "Lawrence is okay, especially when it comes to school stuff. I think I've finally convinced him I just want to be friends. None of this girlfriend-boyfriend stuff."

"Not everyone was as happy with his partner as you were."

"That's for sure! Bob had a fit because he got put with Clovis." K.C. picked up the yellow marker and began outlining the letters. "At first I thought it was because Clovis is new at school, and Bob didn't know him."

"But that wasn't the real reason."

K.C. frowned. "It sure wasn't. At lunch I heard Bob talking to his friends, telling all these dumb jokes about black people. Then I realized he didn't want to be with

Clovis because Clovis is black. How stupid!" K.C. said in disgust. "Why do people think like that?"

Herbie shrugged. "Prejudice has been around for a long time, kid. For some people, the only way they can feel important or smart or capable is to try and make other people feel inferior. Sometimes they choose individuals to belittle—people who are crippled or slow to learn. But often an entire race of people is victimized— because they have slanted eyes or a foreign accent or a different color skin."

"What color is God, Herbie?"

"I bet that makes God mad, doesn't it?" K.C. took out a green marker and began drawing a squiggly border on her cover.

"It sure doesn't make him happy!" Herbie said. "All you humans are equal before God. And if he can accept your differences, if he can keep from pre-judging you based on the shape of your noses or the texture of your hair, then it seems like you could do the same for each other. But it doesn't work that way. Bob can't see past the

color of Clovis' skin, can't see him for the special individual he is. He only sees him as black."

K.C. laid aside the marker and looked at the finished cover, with its bright letters and colorful border. "What color is God, Herbie?"

"Orange."

"Orange!"

"Uh-huh," Herbie smiled. "Orange like summer sunrises and white like December snowfalls and green like the first shafts of newly-planted grass and black like the sky on starless nights and purple like the violets blooming deep in the forest and—"

"Okay, okay," K.C. laughed. "I understand."

"Too bad everybody doesn't, kid," Herbie said, tucking the colorful markers—side by side—back into their box.

* * *

Do not think of yourself more highly than you ought, but rather think of yourself with sober judgment, in accordance with the measure of faith God has given you.
Romans 12:3

Day 30

I can hardly believe it's the last day of school!" K.C. laughed as she walked down the hall, her arms loaded with textbooks to turn in.

"Me either," Herbie said.

"Summer vacation! Boy, are we going to have fun, Herbie. Mom says I can buy a season pass to the lake. I'm going to get *so* tanned! Dad says I'm old enough to drive the tractor this year, so I'll get to be outside all the time. And I'm going to Camp Kickapoo for two whole weeks. You'll love Camp Kickapoo, Herbie!"

Herbie fingered his halo nervously. "About this summer, kid—"

"And Grandma has promised to help me make a quilt from the pieces of fabric she's saved. Won't it look good in my room?" K.C. laughed. "I remember when I thought I'd hate having a bedroom in the attic, but it's worked out fine."

"Some other things have worked out fine for you, too," Herbie said.

"Like what?"

"Well, your grades are good."

"Even math! I survived Mrs. Cannon, Herbie. And Mrs. Martin said my oral book report in English was much better this nine weeks."

Herbie smiled. "I'm not surprised. You've learned a lot this year."

"You mean parts of speech and fractions and stuff about the Civil War?"

"Not just that, kid. You've learned to face your problems. You've learned that God is always close to you, that his Holy Spirit lives in you to help you make the right decisions. You know how to be a real friend and how to resist temptation. You've learned how important it is to pray about even little things and to read your Bible every day. You've learned not to judge other people because of their skin color."

"Or their age," K.C. smiled. "Grandma's okay, Herbie. I'm glad she moved in with us."

K.C. heard the tinkle-clink, tinkle-clink of faraway wind chimes.

As K.C. rounded the corner, she saw Martha standing at her locker. "Martha and I said good-bye last night," K.C. told Herbie. "We promised each other we wouldn't cry at school today. Boy! I sure hate good-byes! Maybe they get easier after you've had to say a few."

"Believe me, kid," Herbie sighed, "they *don't* get easier."

"Poor, Martha!" K.C. whispered as they neared Martha's locker. "Having to leave all her friends and move all the way to California!"

"Yes," Herbie said softly. "She could sure use a new friend."

"Come on, Martha," K.C. said, deliberately bumping into her. "Let's go get rid of these books. My arms are breaking!"

Martha's eyes looked sad, but she smiled. "Sure!"

Herbie watched the two girls walk down the hall. "California," he murmured to himself as he took out his tiny gold spiral and began to write.

The final bell of the day rang, and everyone burst into the hall—laughing and yelling. K.C. saw Herbie standing on the drinking fountain, his tiny gold toothbrush in his hand. "We're all going to the beach!" she grinned. "Judi and Carol and Gene and L.B.—the whole gang! See you later, Herbie!"

Herbie's wings drooped just a bit. "Sure, later." K.C. hurried down the hall. "Take care of yourself, kid!" Herbie yelled after her.

K.C. turned around and waved. "Right!" she called. Then she disappeared into the crowd of kids pushing toward the door, anxious to begin their summer vacations.

Herbie stood watching her for only a moment, then he fluttered his wings and flew toward Martha's locker.

"I must have got a sunburn, Herbie," K.C. said, staring at her red nose in the mirror. "Think it'll peel?"

No answer.

"Herbie?"

The attic was very quiet.

K.C. turned from the mirror and looked around the room. Herbie was nowhere in sight. "Herbie! Herbie, where are you? Somewhere brushing your teeth, I bet," she said as she started toward the door. But her foot hit something lying in the middle of the floor. Her diary! As she picked it up, it fell open to last night's entry. DEAR DIARY, TOMORROW IS THE LAST DAY OF SCHOOL. I CAN'T WAIT! NO MORE HOMEWORK OR ORAL BOOK REPORTS OR MRS. CANNON! I GUESS NOTHING LASTS FOREVER.

Then she saw it—the perfect gold circle around NOTHING. "Herbie!" she whispered, knowing he wouldn't answer. K.C. picked up the diary and placed it on the table beside her bed, next to her Bible. "So long, Herbie," she said softly. "And thanks." A sudden summer breeze stirred her curtains, and through the open window K.C. heard the *tinkle-clink, tinkle-clink* of faraway wind chimes.

* * *

I (God) am with you and will watch over you wherever you go . . . I will not leave you.

Genesis 28:15